Customer Centred

SIGNALLING

Stop selling and start responsible influencing
New insights into online and social B2B marketing strategies

Klaas Fleischmann

Colophon

Customer Centred Signalling. Stop selling and start responsible influencing: New insights into online and social B2B marketing strategies. Practical insights and managerial implications based on academic research. Includes online toolbox and case studies.

First edition, 2018
ISBN: 978-90-827963-0-8
NUR: 163

Author: Klaas Fleischmann MSc Marketing post-graduate Journalism
Editor: Hilde van Halm, MSc Philosophy, MA Journalism
Lay-out & design: Michel van den Boogaard www.de-ontwerper.nl
DTP: StudioS2B at the Grafisch Lyceum Utrecht, The Netherlands
Translation support and editorial support: CumLingua Language & Communication
Publisher: SOIC www.soic.nl

After all the highways, and the trains, and the appointments, and the years, you end up worth more dead than alive.

Willy, Act II, ***Arthur Miller*** *Death of a Salesman*

Preface

Klaas Fleischmann has a wealth of personal experience in the dynamic environment of international business-to-business (B2B) marketing and sales. His experience ranges from small and medium businesses to corporate organisations such as Vodafone, SAP, Canon and Optus Telecommunications. He has also coached and mentored numerous start-up entrepreneurs. Over the years, he has become increasingly aware of the need for further research into B2B marketing, which he believes has lagged behind B2C research for far too long. He is currently a lecturer in Marketing at HU University of Applied Sciences Utrecht, The Netherlands and is working on his PhD entitled 'Bridging the buyer-seller gap in B2B' at the Vrije Universiteit (VU) in Amsterdam. This book gives us an early peek into some of the valuable conclusions from his research.

Having already spent more than a year carrying out a thorough review of almost every publication on B2B marketing of note, and conducting interviews with B2B professionals, Fleischmann is able to provide his readers with unique access to an impressive collection of academic sources. He also supports this book's well-researched seminal theories with first-hand examples.

Fleischmann's research has already concluded that content marketing, inbound marketing and sales & marketing automation have not been able to bridge the buyer-seller gap, and that we are entering a new phase of B2B marketing. One that really does put the individual customer at the core of the marketing strategy.

This is one of those management books that will give managers and students alike plenty of food for thought and enthuse them to apply the latest developments in B2B marketing. Fleischmann takes us on our own customer journey and readers will gain the most by simply sitting down and taking in all the new insights and useful tips one step at a time. The book also includes links to a valuable online toolbox, so that readers can start applying their newly acquired knowledge in their own organisation and projects straight away.

For my wife Annemarie,
and my boys Tom, Joep and Finn
of whom I am so very proud

A note of thanks

Marketing strategy is a crucial element in business practice and needs to be alive in the daily operations of any B2B manager. I have had the opportunity to experience this firsthand while working with a fantastic B2B team at Vodafone. A special word of thanks goes, therefore, to my marketing and sales colleagues at Vodafone, who came with me on a journey to become the then best-selling mobile phone team in the Netherlands. I am still very proud when I think back to those times, the awards we won and the friends I made: Martijn, Menno, Chris, I will be forever grateful to you for allowing me to share the early versions of my agile strategy roadmap method with you. I would also like to thank Berry van de Kooij for encouraging me to start on the B2B marketing track in the first place. Berry, your enthusiasm continues to inspire me.

Special thanks go to Hilde van Halm who has been my personal trusted advisor and sparring partner throughout the whole process of writing this book. Art director, Michel van den Boogaard, who created this beautiful design and, in the process of making this book come to life, has become an even closer friend. The students at the University of Applied Sciences Utrecht and the Grafisch Lyceum Utrecht who helped me with the social media campaign and lay-out of this book. Guys you are fantastic. Studio manager Oscar van der Loo, your advice in trafficking and media management was invaluable. My thanks also go to my editor, Debbie Kenyon Jackson, whose critical comments pushed me to work even harder and helped me get to the point of being able to publish my first marketing book. Last but not least, I want to thank my wife Annemarie and my three super smart boys, Tom, Joep and Finn for giving me the space and time to put my thoughts and ideas onto paper. I am so grateful to have you all in my life.

Klaas Fleischmann

Contents

Figures and tables

INTRODUCTION

A group bell-ringing session marked the end of yet another successful business day. My employer Optus Telecommunications,
a company based in Sydney Australia, allowed us B2B sales reps
who had met their sales target to ring the blunt instrument as
loud as we could. Everyone else around us was shouting loudly:
Optus, yes, yes, yes! I used to be one of the companies high-roll-
ers and back at the office after a day full of cold canvassing
climbed the stage almost every day. After a while the bell-ringing and being applauded to by my colleagues became an addic-
tion. I loved this feeling so much and because I apparently had
a huge talent for selling, Optus became the start of my long and
interesting career in sales and marketing.

Almost twenty years later, that active salesman had died in me. Although I am still
as passionate about sales and marketing as ever, I have discovered how much fun
it is to share my experiences and extensive knowledge with the next generation. As
well as reflecting critically on the effect of traditional market strategies in particular
those that do not integrate and adapt to the role of social media or to the demands
of the online marketing arena. I therefore decided to start a teaching career and to
combine this with PhD research into one of the most important questions in marketing research today, namely how does the buying and decision making process
of the generation Y work? A question that not only interests social scientist, but B2B
marketers as well.

I first became aware of the relevance of this question during my last few years as a
marketing director. I noticed that young B2B professionals didn't want to be influenced by sales people anymore and resisted the traditional marketing ways. Instead
they listened to social media influencers and their authentic and natural messages.
I strongly felt change was coming to my profession. Although at the time I didn't
completely understand what this change would involve, I decided to find out. Now,
two years down the road in my research I am absolutely certain that the era of the

I

bell-ringing sessions is finally coming to an end. The traditional salesman is dying. The power of salesmen and sales departments in B2B organisations is declining rapidly, and we are entering a totally new B2B marketing arena.

Evolution of sales

Over the last fifty years we have moved forward from direct B2B selling of products and resources in the sixties, via consultative selling methods during the seventies and eighties to more target account based selling practices in the nineties and beginning of this century (figure 1). Marketers have only just got used to the notion of content marketing and inbound marketing as the way to attract new customers, establish contact with them and generate more sales through social media, blogs, whitepapers, hotspot downloads. And yet much faster than anyone had expected we're already faced with something new.

Customer revolution

I see the changing B2B landscape in buyer-seller relationships very clearly in front of me. The old decision making unit (DMU) has been replaced by a powerful new purchase organisation: the internet. Like their B2C counterparts, B2B buyers are increasingly embracing social media in order to decrease information asymmetry

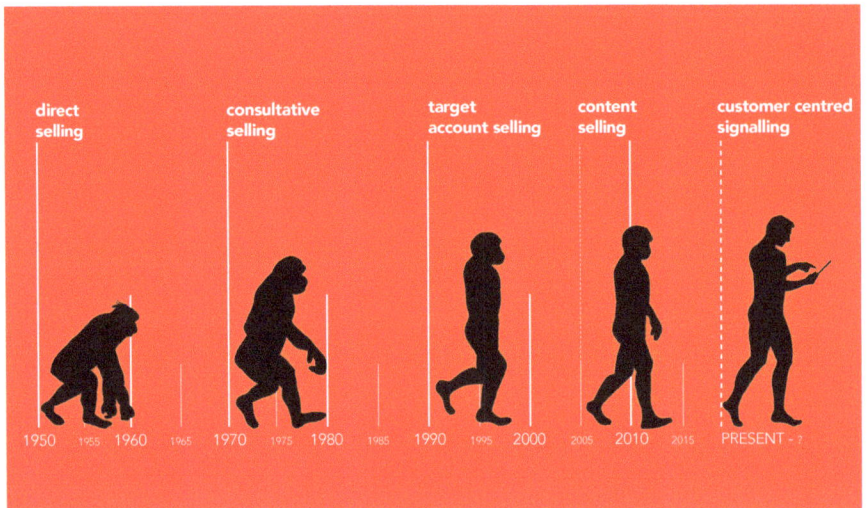

Figure 1 The evolution of sales approaches within B2B marketing communication

12

and reduce uncertainty when selecting sellers. However, customers are increasingly sceptical of 'pseudo-free' firm generated content, and not easily influenced by noisy marketing and sales signals. Hence they move more freely in purchasing decision making than ever before, and are not following marketing campaigns with the behaviour intended by the seller. This is what I call the era of the customer revolution. The era where buyers can only be reached, contacted and attracted by responsible influencing using customer centred signalling. Where confidence in a supplier depends on trustworthy signals. In an era characterized by digital information overload it is all about helping your customer finding their way in this new arena by giving them reliable signals. The era where truthful information exchange between equally powerful parties result in profitable situations for both buyer and seller.

In contrast, corporate social responsibility (CSR) is something different. This term comprises all actions which do not have purely financial implications and which are demanded or expected of an organization by society at large, often concerning ethical, ecological and social issues. Responsible influencing however is a strategic choice companies (need to) make to reinvent their marketing position. A choice whereby they replace hard sales tactics with marketers who try to minimize noise in their online marketing communication efforts, by being truthful about the quality of their products and services. This does not per se mean that the corporation's foundations are based on CSR.

This customer revolution and changing landscape of B2B buying behaviour has created a knowledge gap in terms of how to attract new customers, establish contact with them and how to generate revenues. This is particularly evident in the online B2B marketing arena. As a result, organisations need a new model to help them get closer to their potential customer. Such a business model will ultimately enable management to reduce their company's financial uncertainty. In this book I endeavour to look at the reasons behind the need for transition from sales to responsible influencing. I will introduce a new customer engagement model based on screening, signalling and dynamic customer experience theories that will help you and your organisation understand and address the challenges of this changing landscape. And last but not least, I will show you how to implement these insights in your organisation so that you can maintain your valuable market position.

I

The dynamic customer experience is making forecasting tougher

More instances and touchpoints than ever before are involved in the buying process. The customer experience often begins with a personal encounter at an event, a visit to the website, or on one of the many social media touchpoints. Even news media via reputational storytelling continue to create customer contact moments. The customer views each moment on this customer journey through different lenses, and the effect is much like looking through a kaleidoscope. Their perspective on the product and seller is changing all the time. Even a positive first visit to a website could generate a different reaction on a second visit. As a result, forecasting turnover is becoming increasingly difficult. But all is not lost, simple algorithms are available to replace the traditional sales manager's 'gut feeling'. And tools have been created for you in this book to help you guide your potential customers on their decision-making journey.

Case studies shed light on the critical but susceptible buyer

Organisations are facing the increasing challenge of generating high-quality leads from well-informed but also susceptible and, therefore, unpredictable online B2B buyers. Does the solution perhaps lie in companies reducing over-claiming, increasing their use of paid content, or possibly in stricter governance and restricting the activities of overzealous sales and marketing employees who are creating excessive amounts of content? And what do buyers themselves think? Case studies in this book based on interviews with several international senior managers give us an insight how buyers see their own decision-making process and, critically, what does and does not work for them!

A new strategic roadmap to help identify the best approach to B2B marketing

This book considers the dilemmas facing B2B marketers and sheds light on the best approach organisations and marketers should adopt. The conclusion is clear, a greater understanding of B2B buying behaviour is needed if companies are to deploy their marketing efforts towards the new generation of B2B buyers effectively. This book and the online tools such as the agile marketing strategy roadmap, which have been created to accompany it, make an initial contribution to turning online marketing in the right direction.

Please contribute to make future research possible

I have spent two years writing this book with the aim of educating young B2B marketers so that they can develop their careers. But I didn't just write this book for the new generation, I also wrote it for the old school guys and girls. The number of channels and touchpoints they have to manage today has increased tremendously compared to when they set out as young marketers. Over the years, technology and algorithms have taking over many aspects of our jobs. You might feel that your knowledge and skills have no relevance anymore. This book will change that. There is a need for men and women who understand customer centred signalling and can work with it. And even though the world is a bit more complex than when I was working at Optus, who better than the experienced generation of marketers to become responsible influencers. I hope my book will give you hope and the confidence to be successful in this new day and age.

Finally. I have no commercial interest in selling you this book, but I am happy to take a donation in exchange for a copy of my book so that I will be able to continue my independent research in the next three years. My ultimate goal is to gain a PhD degree in this field. I will use my newly acquired knowledge to share it freely with you via my Facebook, Twitter and LinkedIn channels and via direct contact with my supporters and my students.

The toolkit

This book is accompanied by ready-to-use digital resources. These include:
- an online tool to create an agile B2B marketing strategy roadmap;
- a marketing plan canvas in Excel;
- a loyalty segmentation planning tool in PDF;
- a Prezi or PowerPoint presentation kit.

You will find these and other related resources on signallingthebook.com

CHAPTER 1

The changing customer journey

Managing touchpoints

1

When I first started working as a young marketer for the German software developer SAP I couldn't believe my eyes. As I walked into the sales and marketing department, I saw a Plexiglas ball pit filled to the rim with balls of various colours. It truly fascinated me back then. What was it doing there? I was intrigued that a global brand like SAP appeared to be running its sales and marketing process like an indoor play area. During a B2B training session, a few years prior to my joining SAP, I had been shown a sketch of a container that looked very similar to the Plexiglas ball pit. The main difference being that the sketched container had a funnel at the bottom (see figure 2). They'd left that out at SAP. I think health and safety didn't want lots of balls rolling around the office floor. Much has changed since then and B2B marketing is no longer about simple children's games and funnels - things have become more complex and dynamic - a journey along stepping stones better known as touchpoints. In this chapter I explain how the old system worked and why the new method is better.

Figure 2 The traditional funnel

The sky bridge between sales and marketing

When I joined SAP at headquarters it had a marketing tower and a sales tower connected by a sky bridge. Occasionally, a marketer would stand up from their desk, put down their headset, and throw a new ball into the pit. When the pit was full a colleague would come in, take down the information on a piece of paper, walk across the sky bridge with

1

the list and hand it to the sales manager. Account managers would then phone all the names on the list to make an appointment. Mystery solved: the balls represented potential customers!

Saying a fond farewell to pipeline management

It's hard to imagine, but that's what B2B marketing was like at the beginning of this century. I went on to advise B2B managers for almost twenty years after that using the traditional funnel model (figure 2) with which they too could calculate a reliable turnover forecast. For many years this so-called pipeline management was a lot of fun and more importantly very successful. As an example of this success I would like to mention how the turnover of Dutch PR agency Sabel Communicatie tripled in just a few years' time using this method (see chapter 7). I became an adept for many years until I got to know Professor Anne-Madeleine Kranzbühler. She convinced me, as possibly one of the last converts, of the concept and model of Customer Experience (CE) (see figure 3). So it was thanks to her that I said farewell to my favourite toy. Although, I must say, it was tough!

"SAP appeared to be running its sales and marketing process like an indoor play area."

Don't worry I will explain the Customer Experience concept below. But just to be sure you appreciate why I was so fond of the funnel idea for so long, I will explain my *ball pit algorithm*. Firstly, you attach a fixed probability percentage to each colour of ball (conversion percentage), depending on the average probability that a given colour will generate turnover. For example, a yellow ball has a 50 % chance of becoming an order. You then multiply the estimated value of the order, represented by the size of the ball, by the probability and then by the number of balls per colour. You then add everything together. And there you have it: a sales forecast of what business to expect over the coming months.

As an attentive reader, you will have noticed that my theory assumes that the custom-er follows a fixed trajectory via a single contact point, namely the sales and market-ing employee. However, this view is far too one-dimensional. Today's customers in the pipeline (or from their own perspective: on the *customer journey*) experience the brand, product, service, or even the organisation itself over many different contact moments through various channels. The customer has contact with a B2B brand via LinkedIn, at an event, via newsletters, a vlog or a webpage, etc. I'm seeing more and

"In other words, my beloved simple pipeline algorithm is no longer valid, because we now need to take all of these customer contact points into account when calculating turnover forecasts."

more examples of where individuals send out personal brand-related newsletters, or blog till their heart's content in order to exchange brand experiences outside of the organisation. In other words, my beloved simple pipeline algorithm is no longer valid, because we now need to take all of these customer contact points into account when calculating turnover forecasts.

Dynamic Customer Experience (DCE)

As I'm someone who wears glasses, my brain sees the world through my artificial lenses. Similarly CE is the lens and the customer contact points are the world. The new model (figure 3) describes the intersection between the CE and the individu-al customer contact points. The model argues that my personal attitudes, thoughts, emotions, brand relationship and perceptions determine the strength of the lens through which I view the customer contact, and thus the strength of the CE. As time goes by, my brain collects all these individual CEs and saves them in my memory. The model then explains how my memory puts a second lens over these memories rather like a filter, and thus determines my total CE for the entire customer *journey so far*. But the journey doesn't necessarily end here. As soon as there is a new contact point my entire customer experience may change again. In fact it is highly likely that

1

it will change again. Even if the contact point is the same one as before, I may now experience it differently. Therefore, my CE may become completely different because of that one single contact point. You will have noticed how dynamic this model is.

A new algorithm

I also have to tell you now that not all customer contact points carry an equal value. One customer contact only occurs once, like a visit to a management event, while others occur more frequently, for example logging onto internet banking, or using a popular app. Some contact points have been designed to directly steer customer behaviour, for example to a web page where a customer can leave their email address in exchange for a free download. While others are temporary, such as a one-off visit to a customer experience centre such as the new Nestlé Customer Experience Centre and Museum, 'Le Nest', in Vevey on the banks of Lake Geneva. In short, I can touch different customer contact points for a particular brand at any time of the day or night, but my perception and appreciation of each one will differ each time.

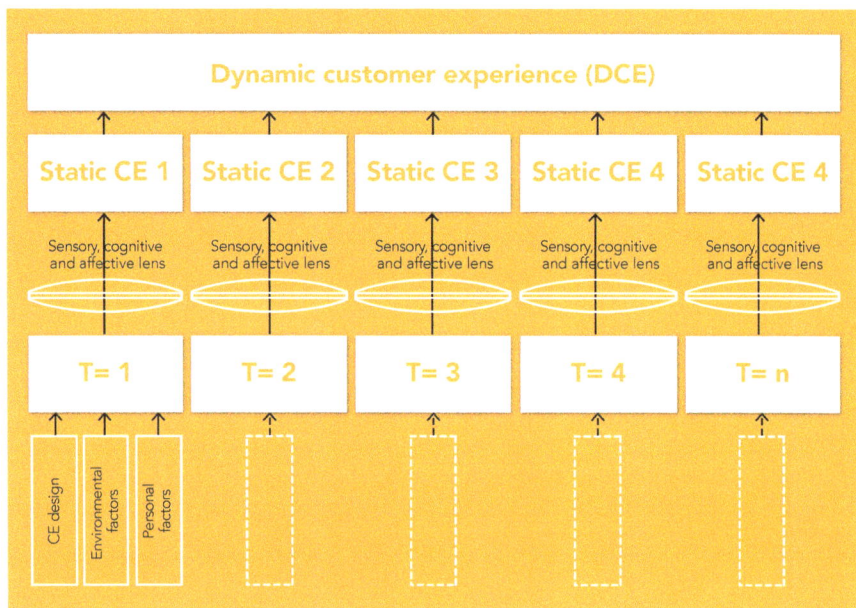

Figure 3 The dynamic customer experience (with permission from Wiley)

The good news is that, by measuring the sensory, cognitive and affective state of mind of the customer, we are able to determine the effect of the lens through which they view each touchpoint on the customer journey. We can then create a new algorithm based on these values with which to calculate the probability of the next step, and ultimately the probability of a new customer.

My new favourite

Because I enjoy radically changing direction (see my LinkedIn profile), I'd like to elevate this so-called DCE theory directly to being one of my favourite models. I recommend that you now use a new algorithm for calculating your turnover forecast: namely the dynamic CE over all the touchpoints (figure 3). I believe this will give a much better indicator for potential turnover in today's world. After all, the forecast for getting a deal using the old indicator was based solely on historical data from the

Le Nest: the new Nestlé Customer Experience Centre and Museum in Vevey, Switzerland
Photo: Klaas Fleischmann

1

CE of a single customer contact point. But that reality is, as I have already argued, totally outdated.

So you need to map out all the customer contact points of your organisation (also known as contact or touchpoint planning). Secondly, you need to measure the lens strength and CE for each contact point you have with your customers through customer insights figures. Thirdly, you then calculate the DCE by multiplying lens strength with CE on each individual touchpoint, sum up and divide the total DCE by a fixed DCE benchmark number. Thus calculation finally yields a success percentage. Based on this individual customer contact data it is, I believe, more than possible to calculate the dynamic CE per customer over the whole customer journey. Ultimately it will be possible to give a prognosis of the outcome of a potential deal. However, this fixed DCE number needs to be based on market research data over a longer period of time and over a large number of touchpoints. Companies will need to invest in this. The goal of my PhD research is to illustrate my point/theory by collecting big data, showing the calculations and comparing them to actual sale results. As a B2B company you can contribute to this research. Please contact me if you are interested.

Conclusion

When I look at it like this, it's much easier for me to say farewell to my old funnel because the ball pit I loved so much hasn't disappeared completely. It's only the funnel vision that's become completely outdated. A multidimensional ball pit 2.0 is on its way and, to coin a popular marketing slogan[1], it will definitely *widen the world of B2B marketing.*

So, the link between my old analogue ball pit game and this new concept of a touchpoint CE is clear. And I'm now thinking the following: if the total sum of all the individual brand experiences determines the CE across the *entire* customer journey, then this means that managing the *dynamic CE* is the most relevant aspect for companies when it comes to managing customer contact. Because a positive dynamic CE determines satisfaction and loyalty in the customer relationship. But, of course, you already knew that!

---

1   Turkish Airlines: Widen your World

The buyer's perspective: Normal buyer Kyle

Key to creating an optimal customer experience is a company's ability to walk in a customer's shoes and understand what makes the journey a pleasant or frustrating one. Although it is imperative for businesses to do their own market research, it is possible for them to learn from each other. Frustrating online experiences show many similarities. Let's learn from my visit to the National Association of Social Workers (NASW) in Washington D.C. This is a non-profit organization providing support for more than 120,000 social workers.

Here I met up with Kyle Northam, working for the division marketing and communication. He told me that NASW had just signed up for business Skype and that all members of staff were supposed to be able to use it. But although they had bought a business package they soon discovered that all individual staff members had to submit personal details before they could activate it. It was a hugely frustrating experience for Kyle as it wasn't solved quickly. He had had to download extra information to help him understand what was required and he had to work his way through and provide extra information from himself. "In the end it worked out, but not before our own tech people came to look at the procedures. The whole thing just wasn't set up intuitively. You had to think like Microsoft. Like a tech person."

Kyle didn't seem to be someone to give up on "tech" easily. He was acutely aware of the need for him to adapt to new technology in order to be able to do his job. But he pointed out that it did ask a lot from him.

"It's a situation where with each new piece of technology or each new application or software, you basically have to learn not only how to use it, but it's almost like you have to start thinking like a tech person. Because a lot of times tech people tend not to think of end users. So, you have to think: okay, why would a tech person make it work this way?"

Kyle points out that this is easier for the generation who have been born and raised in the internet era with technology at hand. But for him, being in his mid-fifties it is a little harder.

CASE

CASE

As the senior administrator in his division part of Kyle's job is to do the main purchasing for the department and staff. In this capacity he will either request goods and items via established channels or he will go online himself and look for things personally. He is thus a frequent B2B purchaser on internet.

Customer dissatisfaction: Too many hoops, keep it simple

Just as he felt frustrated with the extra forms he and his colleagues had to fill out before being able to activate Skype on their individual laptops, Kyle feels frustration when online webshops ask him to do too much in order for him to buy from them. If there are too many hoops to get through before being able to purchase, or it isn't working online and he has to get on the phone after all - that is frustrating. On the other hand if the online transaction is quick and easy and there is a good receipt confirming the purchase the customer experience is satisfying. Kyle points out that he likes things to be simple. But the final moment of truth is if the people in his division are satisfied with the items he has ordered for them.

Searching for a match

Kyle does his best to understand what it is that the staff want (product, price, design). He expects the same from the online companies. "If I'm looking at a thing to buy online, I need to see right there with the object itself, a list of all its specifications that I can read through real quick and make sure that it matches what we're looking for." For the sake of his department he is also interested in how much it costs. If the item is the right price and meets all the requirements it doesn't matter how long it will take to get delivered. These factors are all fairly straight forward. But are there other factors influencing his purchase decision? What kind of information would increase his intention to use or buy a particular item? In his own words: "I'm a sucker for a pretty site. If it's a good site with good images and I can see the item I want clearly. If I can see multiple images of the thing; that assures me that we're actually getting what we want. So, if it's a poorly designed website or the images aren't very clear or it's hard to find the images, then I'm more likely to just ditch that website and go someplace else. Once on the website: I don't want to have to hunt through. I want it to be easy to find. If it's pretty clear, then it's more likely I'm going to buy from that website."

Moving away in seconds

Kyle doesn't want to spend too long searching for needed items. If his initial research (visiting several websites) doesn't pay off because the websites are slow or the images of items on them are unclear, the experience is frustrating. Even though Kyle will move away from a non-functioning website in just seconds, it is annoying if he has to start his search again and again.

If he happens to visit a landing page where a company wants to establish contact with him via a contact form or a pop-up digital agent, Kyle will weigh up his options. If he can tell which information is necessary versus information that is optional, he will remain willing to continue. But he doesn't want to give any more information that he needs to get the purchase done. "I don't want to set myself up to where my inbox is flooded with spam. It's okay to have an email address in there, because otherwise how are you going to get the confirmation of the purchase. But if I'm having to go through a bunch of checkboxes to make sure I don't get any additional emails, that can be frustrating. If a landing page is intuitive, then that's not a problem. If it requires too much, then that's a problem. Or if it's just hard to read, then that's a problem."

Customer care and aftersales

Customer care and aftersales are needed in the online marketing arena. Kyle recognises the B2B is purchasing more and more online. In his personal life it is the same. Some things are not even available in stores anymore. Therefore, in his opinion a smooth and intuitive experience online is critical for maintaining a customer base albeit B2B or B2C. As well as that: "The aftersales are important because nobody buys something forever. So, it comes down to re-assessing when it's time to re-purchase. It's like: do I want to get the same service or not? If the service was too hard to attain then maybe I will go with something else next time."

CASE

CHAPTER 2

Online customer decision making

Screening signals

Pandemonium reigns in the online B2B marketplace as organisations are constantly signalling about their company's quality in order to attract new business. They are using via social media or websites to spread their messages. In contrast, professionals are spending more and more time *screening* the internet. The large number of messages available and the fact that not all of these messages are reliable, make it difficult to select credible quality cues. Authentic customer recommendations for example. New customers like to base their buying decisions on such information. It is therefore essential that B2B marketers understand how buyers prioritise different types of signals and content. This chapter gives you useful scientific information on this topic, as well as an overview of signal definitions and concepts so that you can start using this theory straight away. I also provide you with a couple of simple but valuable tips on how to benefit from screening theory.

New insight into B2B decision-making behaviour shows that buyers are in fact driven by a reliable, professional and consistent flow of trustworthy information throughout their customer journey. Such information may include the number and quality of staff, a business's location, legal status or a company registration with the chamber of commerce. Potential customers, also focus on signals that correlate highly with the product characteristics they are interested in. In academic jargon, these are the signals that 'contain less noise'. In short, buyers try to avoid signals that do not contain relevant information (or, in other words, are 'noisy') since they may lead to errors in buying decisions.

*"Content marketing has become a business in itself.
It's basically advertising."*

Jan van de Ven, CEO Luminext, part of the Eneco Group

When buyers are screening signals (see figure 4) they are looking for signals that are less noisy (for example, warranties or money back guarantees), because these signals are regarded as reliable. Customers view them as being less susceptible to manipulation and mistakes than sales signals. In contrast, sales references or a low or even fixed introduction price are considered to be particularly susceptible to errors and manipulation since these signals are almost always self-reported and often constructed under sales target pressures (accordingly, they are considered to be very unreliable or noisy).

2

Screening signals

Screening theory focuses on the question of how receivers *place differential values on signals*. It argues that buyers select signals that contain a lower proportion of noise, rejecting ones that are not informative about the product or service. Therefore, the *amount of noise* in signals used in the decision-making processes is particularly relevant to you as a manager as it changes *the relative weight* receivers give to a particular signal. It is clear that buyers are becoming increasingly critical.

"We double-check potential partner's contacts on LinkedIn. You can verify the information quite easily. If profiles are completely fake, I would notify LinkedIn and, of course, remove these people from my network."

Yehiel Cohen, Product Manager, LivePerson, Israel

The *amount of noise* consists of two parts: behavioural noise (for example, a company intentionally or unintentionally misrepresenting information about clients, projects and references on their website), and noise due to a weak correlation *or fit* between the signal and the actual quality of the company's products or services (for example, the company is not doing what it claims to be doing). As the quote from Yehiel Cohen, product manager at LivePerson, shows: this also applies to individuals within the company.

Definitions and concepts

The theory of screening is widely used in entrepreneurship, organisational, strategic management and marketing literature in explaining how parties resolve information asymmetry. Signallers or insiders (figure 4) can be persons, or firms. Receivers are outsiders who lack information and would like to receive information, interpret it and possibly send feedback with counter signals.

Feedback can entail either positive or negative private information (e.g. buyers contact information on an online form).

2

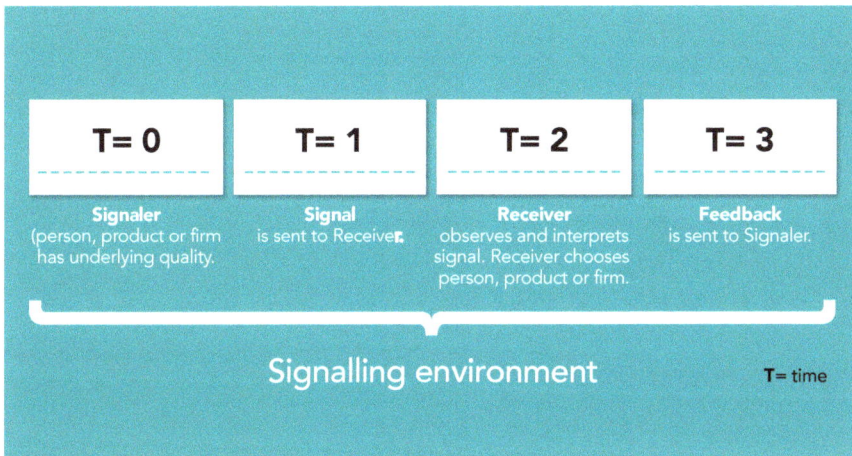

Figure 4 The screening and signalling timeline (with permission from Sage)

The following table introduces an overview of the most relevant definitions and concepts from the theory in order for you to get you start working with these concepts in your own business environment.

Elements	Concept	Definition
Signaller	Honesty (genuineness, veracity)	The extent to which a signaller actually has the quality being signalled.
	Reliability (credibility)	The combination between the signal's honesty and fit (see blow).
Signal	Cost	Transaction cost associated with implementing a signal.
	Observability (intensity, clarity, visibility)	Signal strength.
	Fit	The extent to which the signal is correlated to quality of the signaller. The lower the correlation the higher qualitative and/or behavioural noise.
	Frequency (timing)	Number of times the same signal is transmitted.
	Consistency	Agreement between signals from one source.
	Sale-independent	Publicly visible expenditures before sales when receiver is not easily identifiable (advertising, reputation management, brand name).
	Sale-contingent	Private expenditures during sales transaction, when receiver is easily identified (coupon, low introductory price).
	Revenue-risking	Future revenue is at risk, high introductory price, brand vulnerability.
	Cost-risking	Future cost is at risk (warranties, money-back guarantees).
Receiver	Attention	Extent to which receivers vigilantly scan the signalling environment.
	Interpretation (calibration)	Amount of distortion (definition see below) introduced by the receiver, and or weights applied to signals by the receiver.
Feedback	Countersignals	Responsive signalling from the receiver designed to improve signal interpretation.
Environment	Distortion	Noise that can be introduced by the environment.

Table 1 Definitions of the different elements in the signalling and screening timeline

Conclusion

Both organisations and buyers should be concerned about the amount of noise in signals. Brands should also focus on realising a high correlation between their signal and the quality characteristics of interest to the buyer. If this is not the case, customers will lose confidence in your marketing and sales signals and start looking at higher-quality sellers and/or money-back guarantee information. From the seller's perspective, the counterpart of screening is signalling theory. Chapter 3 will focus on the other side of the coin.

2

CASE

The buyer's perspective: Decision maker Jan

Jan van de Ven is CEO of Luminext, part of Eneco, one of the three largest energy companies in the Netherlands. Luminext supplies dynamic lighting that reacts to the environment using a small IoT (Internet of Things) device. Van de Ven explains how his organisation screens potential suppliers and partners and why he is sceptical about content marketing.

Long-term agreements reduce the need for new buying decisions

We are often intermediary. The final customers are mainly municipalities that buy a complete installation from a contractor and we deliver services and products to that contractor. In this role, we work with a single major partner. We've been co-developing hardware devices with this partner for many years, as part of a long-term relationship that began before I joined the company. This relationship is currently under review as we need to place a new order. It's actually quite rare for us to make buying decisions, because there are long-term agreements in place. So, we just place orders within a framework agreement. In fact, almost everything we buy is within existing relationships.

Within such a long-term partnership, I always try to work on a solution that takes costs out of the supply chain. So, no-one taking on the risk for all the supplies, or having to hold a lot of items in stock. It's all about cooperation. This approach is better for everyone involved.

Taking control of our own buying process

To take control of our own decision-making process we use LinkedIn quite often, especially if I'm meeting someone for the first time. At Eneco, we also use it to check potential partners. We have a venture scouting team that uses various platforms to look for promising start-ups. Patent offices have platforms that are a sort of LinkedIn for companies. We also use the Chamber of Commerce as a source of information. The scouting team then connects all the online information, making it quite easy for us to find a company able to provide a particular technology we're looking for, or an item that's been developed using a certain technology, or a potential partner who's active in a market that we're interested in. We've been using this approach for a few years now, in particular to check out new opportunities.

Price and personal recommendations

By far the most important information that influences my purchasing decision making in general are price and recommendations from someone I know. Content marketing is completely unreliable, I don't trust any online marketing sources at all. For example, star ratings with thousands of people everywhere simply adding and changing information. Content marketing has become a business in itself. It's basically advertising. So, I always feel (even with Google) that the companies with the best price do not make it into the top 5,000 results.

Information that would increase my buying intention, especially when I'm selecting new companies, are the projects they have worked on and the clients they have. Even though I know that these cases and testimonials are often exaggerated, they're a good starting point. But it's important to check them. Everyone likes to put big names on their website, and say they've worked for Google or Microsoft, for example. Of course, this is a reflection on the company as a whole, but it may well have been a different department or a different team within the organisation, and these kinds of references don't always apply to the rest of the company. For example, if you look at a construction company they may say on their website that they've worked on a major tunnel project. But they might only have done the lighting, or even a small component in the fixtures, and yet they present the story as if they built the whole tunnel.

Exaggerations and overclaiming

In addition to exaggerating their role in a particular project, companies often also over-claim about their quality. And, more importantly, overpromise. Buyers need to aware of this. It's like candidates in a job interview, they might not actually be lying, but they're happy to perpetuate a minor misunderstanding.

Good sales people have a reputation for exaggerating a little – with the best intentions, of course. However, overpromising in the belief that 'we'll try to resolve it later' leaves me feeling like I've wasted my time. Because I spent time selecting them and doing my best to make things work. And when things fall apart in a later phase, we only then see that there was a mismatch all along. Because they're not what we were looking for. Bad experiences in the past make me realise the time and risks involved in switching suppliers. So, even if you're not fully satisfied with your supplier, at least you know what you have, and so it's easier to just stick with them.

Annoying digital agents

Websites with specs and features are good for search engines, but sometimes they include a contact form or even a digital agent popping up. They try to talk to you or force you to get in touch. I always find these annoying. I don't want to talk to a computer pretending to be an assistant. I just need a contact button. If I want to get in touch, just give me the contact details and I will decide if I have a clear question or want to send a message. Online forms are also really annoying. I don't want to have to give my contact information just to get a brochure. Why can't I just download the information I want directly from the site?

CASE

CHAPTER 3

Online marketing strategy

Signalling

Now that we have established that touchpoint planning, dynamic customer experience and online screening knowledge is becoming extremely important to reach target customers, the question is how can B2B companies create excellent online customer journeys in order to increase revenues? What I would like to say is this: the answer definitely does not lie with the spreading of 'pseudo free' content on all social media networks. While working at a medium-sized communications agency in the Netherlands, I once made the mistake of making it compulsory for potential customers to fill in their contact details in return for a 'free' download of a whitepaper. In practice I was actually *selling* knowledge (the price being the customer's contact details), rather than sharing it free of charge. This didn't work at all, and we ended up with the lowest conversion rates ever.

Little is written about signalling in academic B2B literature. For example, even Lilien's extensive Handbook of B2B Marketing tells us nothing about dynamic customer experience marketing in B2B. In contrast, B2C marketing seems to be talking about nothing else. The reason behind this knowledge gap in B2B marketing is, in my opinion, a lack of theory explaining the mechanisms that influence online dynamic customer experiences. In this chapter, I therefore take the bold step of using an existing economic theory that I believe gives a very good explanation of how customer experiences can be influenced in online marketing. I will continue to investigate this theory further in my PhD research over the coming years. It is called signalling theory.

3

3

Signalling

When different people know different things about a product or service it is possible to reduce these information asymmetries about your company's capabilities by signalling about them. From the seller's perspective, information asymmetry can exist within two different kinds of information:

1. information with respect to your behaviour or intentions;
2. information regarding the actual quality of your products or services.

Inducing trial

First, let's look more closely at a typical example of information with respect to behaviour or intentions. To induce trial, companies are using Free Company-Generated Content (FCGC) such as blogs, eBooks and YouTube product videos and white papers. This is a clear indication that organisations regard these content examples as being an effective way to find, select and establish contact with buyers. In other words, the content is not posted as truly free, but contains so called behavioural noise and intentions from the seller. Hence, I prefer to call this approach 'content selling'. By which I mean that, even if a buyer does not have to leave contact details behind, the seller will often try to save their digital origins (via an IP address). They may also use cookies to track the unsuspecting buyer around the internet, thus acquiring additional information about their target.

Buyers are seeing FCGC more and more as unreliable sources and are, therefore, increasingly distrusting such content. Why? The answer is simple: because it's *pseudo-free*. Online content is expected to be genuinely free of charge, with no strings attached. All too often, FCGC is not truly free, but is considered to be pseudo-free by buyers. In fact, preliminary results of qualitative interviews carried out with B2B buyers as part of my PhD research show that selling content in return for information (for example an email address) creates aversion rather than brand awareness. In addition it is reasonable to expect that buyers know that they are being influenced by FCGC, which is also referred to as *persuasion knowledge*. As a result, they are beginning to think about the quality of the message before giving an immediate reaction to it, for example by leaving personal details and an email address. Moreover, buyers are increasingly less likely to follow up on FCGC with the behaviour intended by the organisation providing it. They no longer feel the obligation to give something

in return for content because there is a consensus between websurfers that FCGC should, as its name suggests, be free. In addition, surfers value their anonymity on the web. Notice that in terms of the way contact is established with sellers, online B2B buying does not differ significantly from business-to-consumer (B2C) buying behaviour.

On the one hand B2B sellers are using social media, sharing sites, landing pages and online marketplaces to show buyers what they have to offer (for example via specs & features lists, whitepapers, eBooks, online training videos). Buyers will be interested in finding reliable business information as long as they do not have to exchange too much information. They will try and reduce the 'exchange risk' as much as possible, trying to stay anonymous whilst selecting new sellers.

Signal paid or truly free, but avoid pseudo-free signals

Research shows that buyers choose the product with the highest cost-benefit difference. Since FCGC or free versions influence choice, as they decrease cost and increase benefits, suppliers sending zero-price signals will attract more buyers than suppliers sending paid-for signals. Thus, it is important that companies offer genuinely free content instead of pseudo-free versions or buyers will be less attracted to them. Although, it is thinkable that some receivers may treat pseudo-free offers as if they were truly free[2], there is no empirical evidence to show that this is in fact the case. It is, therefore, better to use truly free content in touchpoints in order to create a more effective customer journey.

On the other hand, paid content signals demonstrate a higher quality to the customer. Lambrecht (2016), therefore, suggests that companies charge for online content. Consequently, signalling a free *and* a paid version may allow companies to implement quality differentiation, versioning, or second-degree price discrimination. For example, in periods of high demand, such as during the football season, *countercyclical* offerings with more paid-for content on offerings from popular clubs (paid for business club events, for example) will perform best. So, to ensure customers

---

2   Firstly, the zero-price effect might be better accounted for by affective evaluations than by social norms. Secondly, cost may not be the most important aspect for the buyer. Thirdly, perceived costs may be low or non-existent.

trust their content, B2B marketers need to move away from pseudo-free FCGC towards truly free, or even to paid content as an extra revenue stream.

Signalling unobservable quality

Let us now take a closer look at the second type of information companies signal: the *quality* of products or services. One of the reasons why sellers keep information about their true abilities private, is the existence of *power asymmetries* between different sellers. Power asymmetry is defined as the *ability of sellers to influence the distribution of resources* in a distribution channel, for example by their level of expertise in a certain field or an exclusive partnership with other sellers. Therefore, smaller sellers may on the one hand decide to keep quiet about their true abilities in order to avoid power conflicts that may lead to their higher quality competitor increasing their advertising expenditure. On the other hand, market power asymmetries may give less powerful companies an incentive to *overclaim* their abilities in order to create sufficient new business leads. A good example of this strategy comes from the hotel sector: on overnight business trips you may have noticed that hotel chains and smaller family hotels are located close to each other, next to the motorway. This is because smaller hotels can attract customers and thus increase their revenues, by signalling a high quality comparable to that of the larger hotel chains. Simply by being located near to them. Travellers will then think that the family hotel offers the same high quality as the chain (with the logic that otherwise they would have been out of business a long time ago). So, as long as the large hotel chain is unable to signal higher (unobservable) quality (such as cleaner sheets) the family hotel will continue to thrive simply by being in the right place.

The same logic applies online. Consider the following scenario: a well-known PR and advertising agency claims to have an exclusive partnership with one of the top gurus in the field of user experience (UX). The agency promotes this exclusive partnership heavily online through social media and a special landing page. According to the claim, this exclusive partnership means that businesses purchasing this particular UX service can be sure that the same services are only available through this specific agency and that this service may be regarded as being the best possible in the market. Despite this claim, however, a start-up PR and advertising agency uses the same online channels at the same time to claim that they too are using the guru UX philosophy. They advertise that they can offer precisely the same UX service and quality by signalling that they are part of the guru's partner network. But at a lower price. They did not, however, claim to have an agreement with the guru. Which agency would you contact?

This is a true story, and I know that the start-up company actually obtained more quality leads than the well-known-agency, in spite of the fact that the latter actually did have an agreement with the guru in question. In fact, the well-known agency had a very low conversion rate on their landing page and therefore struggled to make sufficient revenue from this exclusivity deal, whereas the start-up thrived. As the guru received a percentage of the revenue, in the end he not surprisingly revoked the exclusivity deal with the well-known agency and switched over to the start-up company. This is clear practice-based evidence that, in a market without large power asymmetries (pooling market), over-claiming on quality is permitted, as long you are sending honest and reliable marketing signals.

3

Use signalling rather than content selling

It is clear that B2B companies need to shift their current marketing strategy towards signalling rather than content selling to be able to generate enough high-quality leads and stimulate future sales. According to Google buyers are completing half of their purchase decision-making online prior to engaging with a sales representative. This is resulting in empty sales pipelines and financial managers are uncertain about future revenues. Companies are trying to regain control over the B2B buying process. However, they are being led astray by consultants who say deploying segmentation, general branding, or new marketing communication mix strategies (content marketing) alone will do the trick. They are failing to focus on developing individual relationships with decision makers via touchpoints, in order to create an effective dynamic customer experience. That said, companies are also failing to ensure the longer-term loyalty of each customer. This is why it is essential that managers understand the role signalling plays during the overall customer journey.

Conclusion

In order to gain a better understanding of the various signals that form part of the customer journey in B2B, managers need to understand the concept of signalling within the context of information asymmetry and power asymmetry. To this end, B2B companies need to consider the following issues when looking at how and when to use FCGC and whether it is still appropriate to make excessive claims.

- B2B companies need to shift their current marketing strategy towards signalling instead of content selling in order to be able to generate enough high-quality leads and stimulate future sales.
- In a pooling market overclaiming on quality is permitted as long you are sending honest and reliable marketing signals.
- To ensure customers trust their content, B2B marketers need to move away from pseudo-free FCGC towards truly free or even to paid content as an extra revenue stream.

That said, there is in fact an opportunity here for companies to generate extra revenues from FCGC. But to do so they will need a new business model based on the following.

- A better understanding of B2B touchpoint and dynamic customer experience at the start of the customer journey and the online information that influences this phase of their relationship with the customer (see chapter 1).
- An agile strategic marketing strategy roadmap (see chapter 8).
- Better information on where to position themselves in the online marketplace in order to be able to benefit from power asymmetries (see chapter 6).

A business strategy based on signalling theory will help relieve the buyer's tension between selecting a high-quality seller or a low-cost seller. Or, from a seller's perspective: the tension between the objective of obtaining *more* high-quality leads versus obtaining *low-quality* leads. Thus, management will ultimately be able to improve the quality and reliability of their sales leads pipelines and so reduce the company's financial uncertainty.

The buyer's perspective: Decision maker Christiaan

Christiaan Lustig is an independent consultant and entrepreneur with Brayton House in the Netherlands. Brayton is a start-up that he founded together with two colleagues in 2017. The company supports and advises organisations in a digital transformation process by helping them improve their digital platform. Lustig explains his own customer journey when deciding on which online testing software to purchase.

Free trials and optional extras are part of the buying process
The information I need in order to be able to make a decision concerns features. So, if there are two or three options with a tool, I want to know what the options are in terms of features, and what benefits the more expensive option offers above the cheaper alternative. Most suppliers currently have such comparison pages, where they present a list or table with two, three or four options, outlining the features of each one: the cheapest option has these features and not these; the more expensive option has additional features on top of those offered by the cheaper versions. So, I know exactly what I'm getting for how much.

"I believe information from the supplier themselves is of little use."

Christiaan Lustig, independent consultant and entrepreneur, Brayton House

External reviews
Occasionally, I read articles comparing different tools. They provide useful additional information during my decision-making process. If they're about online testing tools, for example, they might compare four, five or even six alternatives from four, five or six separate suppliers. The information that I feel is most useful and most likely to give me the results I'm looking for comes from sources independent of any of the suppliers. I believe information from the supplier themselves is of little use. When you're comparing software products, it's mostly about what features the software offers for what price. I don't really care that much about who built the software and why they built it. For me, it's simply about features.

CASE

CASE

Demo: website versus YouTube

Another source of information that I tend to rely on is demos. A lot of testing tools have somewhere on their own site or on YouTube, click-through and demos of the actual testing process: recorded video screens, how do you do this, how do you do that, how does it compare to other tools…?

Trust

There is a certain level of trust required. Whenever you want to buy, especially online, from a company that you don't know, which is halfway across the world, in addition to the features, the pricing and the overall feel of a site also tend to influence any buying decision. Whenever I feel a product might be superior to other products, but I don't feel very comfortable with the feel of the supplier's site - it needs to feel reliable and dependable - I might consider other options. In a way, this contradicts what I said earlier about not needing the information about a company in order to make a buying decision but, of course, it is important that the site instills confidence based on its look and feel, lay-out, design and general user experience for the visitor.

"I tend to distrust any site that is overly eager to get my contact details."

Christiaan Lustig, independent consultant and entrepreneur, Brayton House

Testimonials

Finally, I often see logos of companies that already use the product. I'm not impressed by those. What I do find interesting though, is a testimonial: a few written sentences on why they use the tool and what they like about it, or sometimes a video of the customer appearing on the screen saying something about their use of the tool. These are things that have helped me make my decision in the past.

Don't interrupt my process

I hate it if a website has cues on their landing page to try to get in contact with me. This could be a form to fill out or, for example, an agent who appears in the screen to talk to you.

In fact, I tend to distrust any site that's overly eager to get my contact details. It's none of their business! Let me do my own comparison and, if you want to have me as a customer, let me browse through your site in peace. Just like I want to browse through a store undisturbed: don't bother me until I ask you.

There are so many sites that after you've scrolled down just half a page or so, bam! there's a pop-up: "Do you want to receive our email updates every day?". No, I do not! Such tactics are hassle and they interrupt me in my own process. These pop-ups sometimes fill up the entire screen, so my attention is diverted from my actual search and I'm forced to focus on this pop-up. On top of that, I also need to be careful what I click on, because there are sometimes even misleading links in the pop-ups saying "Do you want to receive daily updates via email?" and "email address for signing up". Or there's the alternative: "No, I want to stay ignorant forever," for instance. That's a bit of an exaggeration, of course, but these tactics are simply misleading as well as disturbing my train of thought: my buying process.

CASE

CHAPTER 4

Marketing automation

A critical view on inbound marketing

I first noticed the effects of changing B2B buyer behaviour and the trend towards digitalisation on the traditional role of the marketer back in the late 1990s. It was around this time that I started using a pioneering sales forecasting and pipeline management software tool with my sales team at Vodafone. It was only later that the commercial opportunities of this tool presented became apparent. Today it would be hard to find any company using just traditional marketing strategies without any automation in their marketing activities. However, in this chapter I want to take a critical look at this digitalisation of marketing as I believe we need to be more sceptical of its actual benefits. Inbound marketing, in particular, warrants much closer scrutiny.

4

The solution to all your problems?

All too often, managers turn to automation as a means to solving all their problems. Inbound marketing, for example, was also seen by many as the definitive answer to the 64-million-dollar question: How do I reach my customers? Sorry to disappoint you, but inbound marketing is no more and no less than the simple automation of the traditional Hanan approach to consultative selling. In effect, nothing has changed. Inbound marketing is simply an automated tool. Moreover, it brings with it the additional challenge of who will actually fill the systems with appropriate content? Most organisations have neither the budget nor the people to manage these systems properly. This is why they don't work. Conversion experiments show that these systems give no better forecasts than the traditional finger in the air guesstimates of the sales representative they replaced. Those turnover forecasts were often based on unsubstantiated figures and gut feeling. And, more often than not, the automated version is no more reliable. This is why we need a new algorithm. Fortunately, help is just around the corner. And, don't worry, the maths isn't difficult. Step 1 on our journey towards a more successful and more predictable customer experience is defining the customer roadmap.

The changing consumer

Surrounded by a group of 'car salesman-type' stockbrokers, Jordan Belfort played by Leonardo DiCaprio in a Golden Globe winning performance, phones a rather naive customer. With two fingers aimed at the phone, Jordan Belfort alias *The Wolf of Wall Street* has little difficulty in getting the unsuspecting client to part with $10,000. The image from the 1980s of a customer as the victim is a tough one, and is one that still seems to control the convictions of some sales managers. But the consumer portrayed in the film no longer exists.

In the middle of 2015 the free Dutch newspaper Metro, led with the headline: Travel by train through the Netherlands for 7 euros. Alex Bondor, a programmer, was able to by-pass the Dutch Railways (NS) by selling on group-travel discount tickets through his website. With 17,000 registered users, Bondor managed to save himself and his fellow travellers tens of euros per trip.

4

Digitalisation in B2B content

Clever purchasers in the B2B market first consult search engines, various blogs, vlogs, social media channels and digital white papers before making new purchasing decisions. From the customer's perspective this seems like the ideal situation. In the past they would have spent considerable time getting advice from various sources; running the risk of not immediately receiving the correct information. These days answers to complex questions are just a couple of clicks away. Buyers have immediate access to the latest digital B2B content via online self-service without any human interaction. And often for free.

The struggling marketer

Amidst this digitalisation, the traditional marketing mind-set is a sinking ship. So, it's no surprise that we marketers are struggling. We need to adapt in order to completely understand and utilise the new digital marketplace. The effectiveness of advertising has near enough halved over the past fifty years. It has become increasingly clear in recent years that excellent service is more important than slick advertisements when it comes to securing customers.

Big Data and inbound marketing

Digital distractions based on saved persuasion profiles, for example in the form of Big Data, seem to be turning the world of online marketing upside-down. Marketers are now able to use an entire collection of pull-marketing and communication strategies, processes and -technologies[3] aimed at guiding existing and potential clients towards relevant goods and services. The aim is of course to tempt them into starting a relationship online or offline with the provider of these goods and services. This is the latest addition to the *inbound marketing mix*.

To be able to successfully implement the inbound marketing mix, organisations need to have three things in order.
1. Regularly create relevant and convincing content.
2. Own, or have access to online distribution channels such as blog sites or social media pages.
3. Establish and maintain an online community in order to be able to communicate and engage with customers about content.

The B2B purchasing decision making

The rationale is that this new digital marketing communications mix fits perfectly with how B2B customers make purchasing decisions, namely via search engines, by reading blogs, downloading whitepapers from websites and by being active on social media. At first glance this approach seems to be the solution to the dilemmas that so many marketers are struggling with. Moreover, leads generated in this way are five to seven times cheaper than those generated using traditional methods. This model also works well with highly complex B2B services. For example, customers purchasing a service that needs some effort to understand, such as enterprise design, are more likely to refer first to digital content like blogs, podcasts, webinars and slides that the supplier has put online, in order to become more knowledgeable on the topic.

---

3   A commonly used term for this is inbound marketing. Unlike inbound, the alternative - outbound marketing is based on mass-marketing in the form of advertisements, commercials, telephone lead generations, cold calling and telemarketing etc.

However it seems to be cheaper, I am highly critical of this model, for the following reasons.

1. It is based on the principle that customers are targets that need to be guided as leads through a kind of *sales funnel*. As a result the approach appears to be in conflict with a fundamental principle behind customer experience and touchpoint planning, namely that customers want to enter into a relationship with organisations and are partners and not prospects.

2. Little is known about which factors influence the performance and valuation of digital B2B content. For example my own 12-month trial with a website, where the person looking for advice could download a whitepaper in exchange for their email address, generated a conversion of 2.89 % from 5,149 unique visitors and 1 concrete physical follow-up meeting. So, having to leave behind an email address seems to actually damage the performance of digital B2B content. Moreover, visitors also often leave behind fake email addresses.

3. Filling inbound marketing systems with good content needs a lot of additional marketers and, therefore, personnel costs will rise quickly.

4. Inbound marketing is not new. It has been around since the 1970s, under the more well-known name of consultative selling or *Hanan formula*. The salesperson communicates as an advisor and sees the customer as a partner rather than as a customer[4]. But in practice this method only seems to work well in personal interaction and not in the digital B2B processes.

Conclusion: Reinventing the Hanan-formula: the foundation of a new marketing mindset

With consultative selling, the traditional buyer-seller relationship is replaced by a win-win relationship with customers. This relationship is focussed on improving the added value and return on investment for both sides. Hanan's thinking is still very relevant in the new marketing arena. Thus, the future of marketing communication lies also in a model in which marketers work together with the buyer. It is also important that consumers are able to share in the profits generated by marketing. That is what

---

4 Together, the customer and the advisor draw up a so-called Profit Improvement Proposal (PIP). This PIP has value for both the customer and the advisor, because the customer doesn't need to pay, but rather, by investing in the future, will actually increase profits.

Hanan saw in *B2B marketing* back in the 1970s. Yet relatively little research has been carried out into such a model with respect to digital B2B content.

This book introduces such a model in chapter 7, the so-called customer engagement model for B2B. One that is based on responsible influencing and retargeting (see chapter 6). This is because I know that you are probably struggling with these issues. You don't know how and when to come into contact with new customers. This lack of knowledge and insight can result in an empty sales pipeline, leading potentially to uncertainty with respect to the continuity of the company. '

My new model will enable managers to:
- plan and understand multiple touchpoints with customers;
- manage the dynamic customer experience much better;
- understand the customer journey within the B2B content marketing context much better;
- respond to the customers' digital information requirements;
- understand when content needs to be free, and when the customer is willing to pay for it.

4

But first I want you to look at the most important starting points in this new model. That is your branding and your reputation management. Because if these are not managed well, the new marketing model will not work. In his final words in The Wolf, Jordan Belfort underlines the importance of maintaining trust in business. Just before he goes to prison, he says: "never accept a less than satisfactory answer and never let anyone lie to you."

CHAPTER 5

Branding

The company or brand suffering from a bad reputation? Get rid of the CEO!

Amid the scandal of the manipulated emissions testing software for diesel vehicles, there's a deeper story about brand confidence. After all, we all know the dilemma: when writing texts for PR or advertising, should you make products out to be better than they are or just be completely honest? Should you stick closely to the message of the quality brands and claim that your brand is just as good for fear of losing your customers to the competitor.

Signalling theory (see chapter 3) claims that this tactic will pay off if you don't push it too far. Low-quality brands benefit from the campaigns of higher quality brands unless, of course, the buyer finds out that they're exaggerating or are deliberately providing incorrect information. This will naturally result in a loss of consumer trust. Research shows that in the wake of fraud, stakeholders evaluate businesses differently - using stricter criteria than before. What's more, it will become clear that firing the CEO is helpful.

When is a 4-star hotel not 4-star?
There is a proven, irrefutable link between advertising and the client's perception of product quality. In those situations where buyers have insufficient information about the brand's quality to enable them to choose a supplier -that is, there is information asymmetry - (see chapter 3), brands take the lead in showing that they are offering high-quality products or services. This is for example, the case with intangible services such as project management or consultancy. Moreover, to gain a competitive edge or to keep stakeholders satisfied, company board members are tempted to paint their business affairs as being more promising than they really are. This, of course, only works until these untruths are discovered. The outside world judges the culprits harshly for their overly favourable presentation of their position. Low-quality brands in particular exploit such situations, but only for as long as the exaggeration is not discovered or the cost of competing with the high-quality brand doesn't become too high.

5

Brand confidence lost? Customers turn to other information

The reliability rating of corporate communications depends on the amount of noise contained in the message (see chapter 2). This noise is generated on the one hand by the possible mala fide behaviour of managers and on the other hand by actual poor quality. For the sake of convenience, I will focus on the first form of noise in this chapter. If a board spreads unreliable information about their brand for example financial restatements of earnings (or hotels for example, deliberately pretending to have 4 stars when they only have 3) and that information is factually incorrect, once stakeholders discover the deception, the brand's reputation is not only damaged (a logical result) but customers also seek out other sources of information about the company.

Firing the CEO does help

In such cases of deception the reputations of the company's directors become the subject of further scrutiny. Following a breach of trust, the way the outside world

5

"My most urgent task is to win back trust for the Volkswagen Group - by leaving no stone unturned."

Matthias Mueller, the new CEO at Volkswagen

views a brand, changes and this has an adverse effect on the process used for brand evaluation. For instance a customer may suddenly tell an account manager that in spite of their excellent personal relationship, they're moving over to a competitor as a result of the management's dishonesty and the resulting bad reputation. In such a case a brand can only revive its reputation by coming forward with honest information as soon as possible. Depending on the severity of the wrongdoing stakeholders will then, sooner or later, resume using their standard evaluation criteria. But if there has been an extremely serious breach of confidence the only remedy will often be to get rid of the person who is ultimately responsible: the CEO. If we look at 'dieselgate', the row over the departure of Volkswagen CEO Martin Winterkorn could have been avoided if the company had been completely open about the fraudulent emission testing software much earlier in the process.

Tip #1: Stay true to your word

Corporate branding is the pivot point between marketing and corporate communications. All actions in the strategic marketing roadmap should be based on brand identity - based on your corporate values, mission and vision - as a starting point. In other words, if your organisation believes in sustainable packaging then all future actions in your distribution chain need to be based on that belief. In contrast if identity and marketing actions are not aligned, dieselgate could well happen to you.

The extent to which a company lives up to its identity is called reputation. Or, as the owner of a medium-sized communications agency in the Netherlands once explained to me: *it is those things a customer says about you when you are outside the room waiting.* Reputation is the way companies are seen and appreciated by its stakeholders such as clients, employees and politicians.

Hence in order to maintain a positive reputation, a company needs to fulfil its promises. Everything a company does, will be scrutinised by customers and influence their decision-making process when buying from that company.

"Your brand is what other people say about you when you are not in the room"

Jeff Bezos, founder of Amazon.com

5

Tip #2: Implement real-time reputational management

Bertwin Tiemersma accountability and issue manager at Achmea once explained it like this to me:

'' Marketing insights empower a business to influence its reputation. Real-time analysis and reputational data coming from solutions such as social media monitoring tools, or RepTrak® tools enable companies real time to continually improve their reputation. Measurable results make a significant contribution to ensuring identity and strategy in three phases:

Phase 1: Take stock

Taking data stock starts with formulating a *problem statement*, or a SMART KPI. Based on this, you should determine what information you need to make decisions. For example information on target groups, engagement data (see chapter 1), issues, or the extent of influence certain stakeholders have on your business. Finally, you complete this stage by carrying out desk and field research. Of course, you need to check all the data for significance and degree of relevance.

Phase 2: Analyse

Use the management methods (see figure 5) to provide insight into the extent to which your organisation controls its reputation, employee involvement and/or specif-

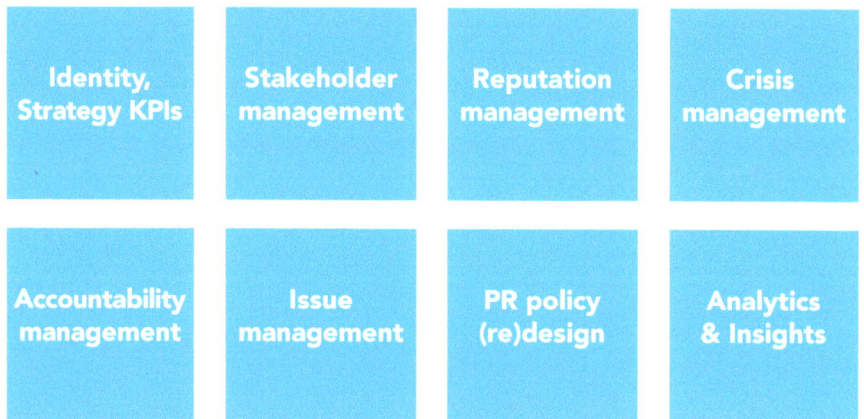

5

| Identity, Strategy KPIs | Stakeholder management | Reputation management | Crisis management |
| Accountability management | Issue management | PR policy (re)design | Analytics & Insights |

Figure 5 Issue, reputational and engagement methods

ic issues that arise. These methods will also help you analyse the extent to which data from the touchpoints support your current marketing strategy.

Phase 3: Adjust

If alignment between identity, reputation and marketing strategy is poor, you need to formulate a new marketing strategy as soon as possible."

Conclusion

If you have implemented real-time reputational management in your branding approaches but are still being confronted with unexpected issues, my advice is to admit your mistake as soon as possible and offer your apologies. The sooner companies show remorse the sooner stakeholders will forget the incident and go back to *business-as-usual*, reverting to using the standard criteria for supplier selection as they do so. Of course this may not apply in extreme examples of damage to reputations such as in the case of Volkswagen. Here, the only remedy was to get rid of the person responsible as soon as possible and start again with a clean slate.

5

CHAPTER 6

Social marketing

The importance of boosting, influencing and retargeting

I once overheard a conversation between the CEO of a company and a rather bright consultancy manager. They were discussing how the latter's eager employees were posting stories and content on social media. The consultancy manager was defending her staff's social media efforts because, in her opinion, social influencing was important for future growth of the business. Her reasoning was that the company needed every extra touchpoint in its efforts to reach new customers and create more brand awareness. The experienced CEO simply shook his head and said that consultants need to be billable and shouldn't waste time and money on useless social media activities. He had the more powerful position in the company and so he won the argument that day. But for me it was a clear example of why companies need to start the discussion about who should and should not get involved in social media influencing. This chapter is for all those professionals who still need to convince their management of the importance of social media in the B2B marketing mix.

6

Who are social influencers?

There are many definitions of the term *social influencer*. For example, an influencer is an individual who has the power to affect the purchase decisions of others because of their real or perceived authority, knowledge, position, or relationship with the customer. Or the *independent third-party* endorsers, who shapes audience attitudes through blogs, tweets and the use of other platforms. Similar a company's marketers and sales employees who - out of eagerness, self-interest or lack of governance - are using social media to publish content with the aim of establishing contact with potential customer are also a different type of social influencer. They are decreasing the need for traditional cold calling

Authentic

By participating on social network platforms, such as Facebook, Instagram and YouTube, social influencers are able to increase their popularity. The content they share in blogs and online videos enables them to get their message across to a wider audience. As many social influencers create their own content with personal stories, they are often seen as more 'authentic'. Another advantage is that social influencers generally tell personal stories. This enables their online followers relate to them more. The *peer status* social influencers often have, give buyers a sense of trust in them that is comparable to an independent third-party endorser.

In fact, buyer confidence in brands has shifted from authority figures to average people, just like you and me. Buyers no longer want to hear neatly packaged marketing messages, but prefer to be engaged or to proactively engage in conversations. Moreover, the line between social media relations and public relations is becoming increasingly homogenous with brand strategy as the foundation that builds authentic relationships.

Social influencers and B2B brands

An effective way of identifying relevant bloggers is by using a valuation algorithm that seeks to find the degree of a blogger's influence. Booth and Matic, for example, identify the following variables in order to create this new algorithm:

- viewers per month (VPM): number of visits to the blog per month;
- linkages: popularity of blog post links inbound and outbound;
- post frequency: volume of posts per given time;
- media citation score: volume and level of media that cites the blogger;
- industry score: that is the number of industry guru points based on industry events;
- social aggregator rate: level of participation in the social web (for example, Twitter, other bloggers/blog communities, LinkedIn);
- engagement index: reader response and the quantity of comments;
- subject/topic-related posts: volume and immediacy of subject/topic-related posts;
- qualitative subject/topic-related posts: qualitative review of subject/topic-related posts;

- index score: identification and rank of the influencer in the social web based on the above-mentioned variables.

This method provides a strong framework for marketers to follow when measuring both quantitative and qualitative influence impact.

Impact

The capacity of social influencers to impact customer behaviour depends on three Rs.

1. **Relevance**: or focus on what aligns with the brand. It is important that the influencer is able to create authentic content, share first-hand stories and post quality photos.
2. **Reach**: maximise the reach without compromising the remaining Rs. But do not just look at reach as a way to get the message out there; it still needs to be relevant and engaging in order to create value.
3. **Resonance**: the difference between celebrity and everyday influencers is that a celebrity does not respond to every fan. That is why everyday influencers can be more powerful in terms of promoting your brand if you provide a conversation and engage with the audience.

From my own interviews with professionals in the field it follows that in B2B, relationships are also key. In the sense that the influencer is authentic and shows that they are truly excited about sharing the experience.

6

A trusted peer

The value of social influencers for a brand is, therefore, that influencers inspire their fans and followers to purchase products and services. Firstly, a Nielsen survey shows for example that 81% of the fans purchased a product because of the recommendations of a social influencer. Secondly, a personal connection with the author is the most important buying motive based on influencer's content. That is, customers look at content of online influencers in the same way as they engage with others in a face-to-face conversation. Thirdly, people want a personal connection. Consequently, the use of social influencers provide brand marketers with the possibility of joining conversations. Social media give brands direct access to engage in conversations that build relationships and encourage brand loyalty. Although brands cannot completely control a conversation, they can steer it by using social influencers as their brand advocates.

Social influencer theory

The first theory that helps us understand why influencers are influential in the first place is the theory of Social Learning. This theory states that individuals can learn and acquire new patterns of behaviour via observations, imitation, and modelling. Bandura identifies three necessary stages: (1) attention; (2) retention, and (3) motivation. He also suggests that behaviour is either deliberately or inadvertently learned. Social media influencing fits this theory as influencers reinforce and recommend products or services they like, via blogs and videos. Readers or viewers are then likely to adopt these behaviours or opinions about a product, copying the influencer.

Effectiveness of Word-of-Mouth marketing

Another way to describe influencer marketing is by looking at Word-of-Mouth (WoM) marketing. WoM describes the process of face-to-face communication between people without commercial intent. It has also been defined as the communication between customers about a product, service, or a company in which the sources are considered independent of commercial influence.

Internet has caused a shift from offline to online WoM, where people can talk freely about anything they like. This electronic form of WoM often occurs between strangers. WoM has proven to be more effective for brands as it is considered more credible and trustworthy. They argue that the more customers attribute the communicator's review about a product to that product's actual performance, the more the consumers will perceive the communicator to be credible. And the more confidence the consumer has in the accuracy of the review, the stronger their belief that the product has the attributes mentioned in the review.

Brands need to use the little influence they have to keep online conversations positive. That way they are able to persuade others to try the product. Influencers have a strong position in forming the opinions of the audience regarding products, whereas the brand can only influence the tone of the conversation.

How to use influencer marketing

Implementing influencer marketing has been a hot topic in many B2B industries over recent years. As mentioned above, social influencers can help brands join online conversations, and give access to engagement on a new level with target audiences. Brands really should, therefore, start to use social influencers. In order to select suitable social influencers, marketers should consider the relevance, reach, resonance and relationship of the social influencer with the audience. When these four criteria align with the brand, the social influencer is more likely to inspire their followers to a purchase decision.

Reaching people other channels don't reach

One excellent example of a former sales manager who transformed himself into a very successful social influencer is Canadian B2B sales person Marc Binkley. He argues that a brand can use social influencers to penetrate the daily lives of the target audience in an organic way. This means that the brand is able to expose the target audience to images, videos or articles about services and products on a frequent basis without sending out too many marketing messages through conventional channels. Social influencers also enable a brand to reach people they would otherwise not have reached.

Furthermore, by using social influencers the brand is able to create new digital touchpoints (see chapter 1) with the target audience. And because the younger generation in particular use social media frequently, brands can now reach out and secure future audiences as well. It is evident that social influencers have influence on all of the following levels of the AIDA-model.

- Creating product or brand awareness.
- Creating attention.
- Creating desire.
- Creating action.

Creating product or brand awareness

There are three key aspects regarding the creation of a product or brand awareness.

1. The influencer's image needs to fit with the imagery of the brand.
2. It is not necessary for the social influencer to use the brand for a long period, but they need to create content as soon as possible.

3. Creating awareness needs to be oriented on creating *recognition* amongst the target audience rather than creating *recall*. For example, we can see that increasing numbers of people recognise products more easily after having seen or read about them via social influencers.

Creating attention

When the focus is on creating attention, social influencers should post content about a brand for a longer period of time so that their audience will start to associate the brand with them.

Creating desire

To create desire the social influencer needs to have a high level of credibility. The audience needs to believe that the influencer is talking objectively about the product. However, this can be difficult to achieve with some target audiences. Older buyers for example are more sceptical about the influencers than the younger generation. This may be due to the fact that buying intention decreases as the audience gets older. Older customers look for additional information. The contribution of the social influencers for this group is, therefore, lays mainly in creating product or brand awareness and attention.

Creating action

Although there are people who only want to *consume content* about brands, one type of influencers has a significant influence on creating *action*. This is the case when influencers are considered by their audience to be *opinion leaders*. For those influencers, the majority of their audience not only want to see or read a review from them but also want to ask him/her about their user experience. Thus, opinion leaders have a high level of authority and credibility among their audience and are therefore able to influence decision-making processes. For example, customers may ask them questions about what they think of a brand when they are in doubt and take their answers into consideration in the purchase decision.

Two types of social influencers

From the above, it is possible to conclude that there are two types of social influencers.

1. **Brand boosters**

These are the social influencers with a large audience but with a lower level of credibility. They are good in building awareness and recognition. Often, they create content for several brands and can be considered as social advertisers. It is important to bear in mind that brand boosters are not necessarily brand loyal. For example, a consultant working at an organisation could quite easily blog about other solutions than the ones from his own brand in case they are good. They will naturally incorporate this into their article, blog or vlog they are producing. Companies should enable brand boosters to create such content.

Advantage

An advantage of the brand booster is that, because they come into contact with several brands, they can combine brands from different industries in their content. This enables brands to contact an even broader audience and send their message out to people they would otherwise not have been able to reach.

2. **Influence champions**

These are the social influencers with a high credibility who are seen by their audience as opinion leaders with a high level of authority on a certain topic. They can acquire this high level of credibility by being brand loyal, which often involves some sort of contract to determine agreements and expectations regarding content. Or by being seen as highly objective. These influencers have more influence on the decision-making process than the brand boosters and give more in-depth information about the brand, rather than just on their user experience. Because they give more in-depth information, they are good in creating recall and making brands top-of-mind for future decision making.

6

Advantage

The advantage of using influence champions are two-fold. Firstly, the short-term impact that involves creating recognition amongst the target audience for both the brand and the product. For example, in rebranding and introducing new products and services the brand should first focus on creating product or brand awareness. Secondly, a long-term impact focused on creating recall and making the product top-of-mind.

The need for additional digital touchpoints

My research thus shows that short-term and long-term impact require different types of social influencers. It is also important to note that, as they get older, target audiences become more sceptical about the objectivity of social influencers. That said, if the social influencer is positive, the older audience will go and look for additional information. This is why brands should deploy additional digital touchpoints.

Include social influencers in touchpoint planning

As shown above, the power of social influencers should not be underestimated. They play a significant role in the changing B2B online landscape. Organisations should, therefore, account for the conversions that arise from social influencer content in their touchpoint planning and customer journey management. (See chapter 1, 7 and 8 on how to do this.) The approach will vary, depending on the phase in the product life cycle:

Early stages

In the early stage in the product life cycle, I advise organisations to focus on creating product awareness through brand boosters. This establishes a level of recognition and makes customers enthusiastic about tangible benefits. For example the salesforce, marketers or other employees could start blogging new content about the innovative capabilities of the brand. And remember when introducing new content, it is important to use every channel possible to spike product awareness.

Growth phase

In contrast throughout the growth stage of the life cycle, the focus shifts to conveying knowledge about non-tangible financial benefits such as return-on-investment. This is done by using influence champions. However, in this phase of the life cycle the level of product awareness also needs to be maintained. So, brand boosters should keep posting about the brand as well.

Maturity phase

As content progresses through the lifecycle into the maturity phase, the content influence champions need to convey information about non-tangible, non-financial benefits like interesting corporate stories. This will help build a strong and positive reputation.

Decline phase

Finally in the decline phase of the product lifecycle as the level of exposure drops and conversion becomes more difficult, the brand needs to shift influencer marketing efforts towards an appropriate *retargeting strategy*. By definition, retargeting is the practice of reaching web visitors after they have left your site. It involves systematically engaging customers who didn't convert (that is, buy a product or service). This is done via email, advertisements and other media (that is, digital touchpoints) aimed at converting this group into solid leads. For example, you can plan all possible touch points accordingly in advance. Research shows that customers who receive retargeted ads and communications are 70 % more likely to convert than those who experience no retargeted content. Software developer Adobe, for example, found 25 % of consumers likes receiving retargeted ads because the content reminds them of products or services they have viewed in the past. In addition, conversion within older target audiences increases, because older people look for more touch points than millennials before they are convinced.

Conclusion

B2B managers need to accept that social influencing has become as strong a marketing communication strategy as PR. Therefore, they need to facilitate their employees in becoming social influencers themselves, with time and budget to create articles, blogs or even vlogs. At the Dutch Rabobank, employees are actually using internal vlogs to generate involvement for new ideas. Why not empower marketing and sales to do the same externally via a personal account? Employees who become influence boosters are an important first step on the way to new online marketing because they add new digital touchpoints with which to create brand awareness and influence future buying behaviour. The second step is to connect your brand to influence champions. Finally, make sure to reach your visitors even after they have left your site. Hence, retargeting is key in social influencing strategy because it creates engagement with both younger and older customers who did not convert during their initial contact.

6

A buyer's perspective: Decision maker Jack

Jack Niama, an independent trade consultant and businessman with expert knowledge of Ecuador, Latin-America described to me how even after having made an initial choice for a product or company a bad peer review on a vital topic such as social responsibility could make him completely change his mind about buying from the company. Apart from social responsibility there are many more issues that provide crossroads in his online decision making journey. All of which are guided by his main focus namely, deciding whether or not a company is reliable enough to do business with.

The search for reliable information

Working from the Netherlands, Niama is dependent on using the internet to his advantage. And he uses it extensively and intensively. At the outset of his research he will throw his search net wide and far via Google and see what comes up. As his initial hits come up he is forced to become more specific and accurate as to what he is looking for.

Once he has found companies that can provide him with what he is looking for Niama will make a shortlist of potential sellers for himself and start digging a bit further and also use official sources such as the International Trade Centre or trade organisations/sector associations. The ITC provides Niama with many facts and figures that he needs. Whilst the trade organisations/sector associations will give an insight into which suppliers are members. These are usually the largest businesses with the most potential. "At least, this is true in the sector that I work with. For me, that is quite an important source to get an idea who the main players are." After this initial search Niama will send for product samples and look at product videos via YouTube. At this stage he will also check out what other buyers think of the product by looking at their websites for comments or visiting review websites. But he will also talk to expert consultants offline from his own business network. Of course, he realises that their information maybe a bit biased or coloured, but that doesn't matter because it still provides him with up to date information on what is up and coming. "Most of them also have blogs or articles on a particular product or service. You kind of learn what the latest trends are and what they're working with. This is the kind of information I look for which you can use in your purchasing decision."

Niama is also positive about other non-automatised opportunities that a company may offer him to gain information about them and their product. For example if a company

CASE

website enables him to have a live chat with a company representative. It is the next best thing to having personal contact over the phone, something that Niama still prefers. A last resort would be filling in a form online and waiting to be contacted.

Getting closer to the decision point

As he continues researching the companies he is interested in Niama tries to get closer to the companies. He may for example check out who is behind the company, what is their experience, do they come from that sector. Information that he can find on LinkedIn for example. "That is maybe a step further which I would need if I'm getting closer to the decision point and you're really in doubt, so you want to go more in-depth."

The more transparent a company becomes for Niama, the better. If a company is active on social media sharing and publicising information about its activities that is a good thing. Not only does it provide him with information, it is also an insurance policy that if he has something to say about the company or it's products there are lines of communication available to him that will make a difference.

"Now I'm relying more on that information as well, so that's the one thing that I check back and forth. It's not only Google search and the websites, but now I'm also looking for social media activity, because that also gives me an indication... first of all, it gives me more personal information about the company. It makes the company a little more transparent. It shows how many followers it has, how many people are looking at them, so it gives you little bit of an idea how large, how much they are not shy about sharing their activities, because they're quite confident."

Niama points out that if a product is already standing up to his scrutiny through positive testimonials, social media is another layer that can back it up and make him more confident about the product.

However, even at this stage having got so far with a company Niama will still keep his channels open for negative news as well. This, like every other step in the decision process, influences my decision making. It's almost like adding or subtracting one point from the total score.

Keeping in contact: the personal connection

"It's always nice to have quick news updates with photos, but not too extensive. Something that you don't have to spend a lot of time reading on, but something that lets you know what the company is up to today or that they're having a promotion soon. Facebook and Twitter are the two platforms that I look at for this. I always have a quick look on if a company has these two. Maybe there's information on this, that I wasn't looking for, but gives me new insights. I always like the visual part, photos for examples, and the personal connection they try to give or that you have with the company."

CASE

CHAPTER 7

Customer engagement

Introducing a new model

In this chapter, I will compare customer engagement to the dating process. The success of the new journey organisations need to go on with their prospective customers is no longer determined by the traditional account manager and his sales-rep approach, but by multitude of online contacts. Let's see, who needs to get involved with and how the contact with the customer is to lead firstly to an *engagement*, and ultimately to a long and happy *marriage with your brand*?

Dating advice

The ancient Greeks realised that temptation and trust go hand in hand. The Greek goddess Peitho (goddess of persuasion and temptation) has close links with Aphrodite (goddess of love). Statues of the two goddesses were often placed next to each other so they could 'chat'. With Peitho depicted as Aphrodite's trusted adviser. Let's stick with this thought for a moment: building up trust is an essential part of the early stages of courting. How does this work in customer engagement? And, incidentally, if you are currently not in a relationship you can also take this chapter as a bit of free dating advice.

The odds of rejection

Starting up a conversation straight away (cold acquisition) may mean that you need to rely on special tactics as recipient of the unexpected and unsolicited, attention doesn't know you. You could burst into song, like Tom Cruise in the film Top Gun[5], to immediately tug at the heartstrings. The Few individuals however have that special ability that enables complete strangers to immediately trust them and feel some level of empathy towards them. The odds of being rejected are very high.

A second date?

A safer and, therefore, better idea is to hunt in a group as can be seen in the film A Beautiful Mind[6]. John Nash tells his friends, who are all trying to get to the same girl in the bar: "Doing what is best for yourself and doing what is best for our group will yield the best possible outcome for all of us". The idea is that if your friend is standing next

---

5   Paramount Pictures, 1986 (www.youtube.com/watch?v=HVNWSEX-WqU)
6   Universal Pictures and DreamWorks Pictures, 2001 (www.youtube.com/watch?v=2d_dtTZQyUM)

to someone they know and it happens to be a person you're attracted to, start by listening in on their conversation. This could also be a discussion in a social media group. This will help you get to gain some important background information. Ask your friend to introduce you. Someone who is an authority on the topic being discussed could perhaps introduce you to the group. You can then come up with your own fitting questions on topics your potential new contact or date may find interesting. My theory – although not a scientifically tested one – is that this approach will lead to a pleasant and engaging conversation both online and offline, based on a mutual sense of trust. You may have by-passed your friend a little in the process, but you have at least made a positive first impression on his/her friend, and may even get a second date.

Trusted adviser

As in Ancient Greece, trust is still an important aspect in both personal and professional relationships. In all forms of online and offline business, trust and, in particular, the trusted adviser are key. There is a high probability of a trusted adviser being listened to. They open doors, have a stronger network and ultimately get more customers. Master Yoda, for example, in the Star Wars sequels including The Empire Strikes Back is one such trusted adviser.

It is not only the account manager who is able to play this role, but also the project manager, consultant, online specialist or secretary. In fact, anyone with customer contact. For example, I was involved in customer satisfaction research carried out by printing technology company Océ, now a Canon Group company. The research showed that customers of a service are more likely to trust the technical employee who visits every month to replace the toner, than the higher-paid account manager who simply writes quotations. Thanks to the frequent visits, the technical employee not only knows that the customer needs new toner sooner than the rest of the organisation, he is also trusted by the contact person with whom they have built up a relationship - having solved their technical problems for years.

The acceptance of advice from the trusted adviser is very high. The same research also showed that so-called *affective commitment* has a positive effect on the satisfaction and loyalty of a customer. Quotations, contracts, email confirmations (also known as calculative commitment) on the other hand, do not. This means that the trusted adviser is not only more likely to sell than the account manager but also to retain a loyal, satisfied customer, who will listen to their advice.

Authority as temptation strategy

Psychologist Robert Cialdini came up with six temptation strategies, based on research into how the human mind works. One of these strategies is the application of the psychological principle of authority. He based his research on the Milgram experiment from the 1960s. This classic research shows that people are more obedient to a researcher in a white coat (showing authority) than to a researcher in normal clothing. If you apply this principle to professional relationships, we must conclude that the adviser, the authority in their field of work will be more successful in social influencing than someone who does not have a proven track record.

That means that an influence champion who publishes frequently and is regularly in the news will be much more convincing during conversations on social media and have more followers on social media than an ordinary sales guy- or girl. Therefore, it seems worthwhile to build up a position of authority. e.g., via writing blogs or articles.

Proof of the pudding is in the eating

A Dutch medium-sized PR company, proved that this type of customer engagement works. In a period of less than three years, this agency tripled its turnover when a group of advisers started working with this approach. The team quickly made significant steps thanks to workshops, roleplays and on-the-job training in what they referred to as *consultative engagement*. According to the company's founder, this success was thanks in no small part to the willingness of the group's eager learners to listen to each other's feedback. Using video recordings of customer engagement on different touchpoints they were able to improve their consultative engagement. This structured approach produced a new unity in the approach of the customer journey process as employees learned from one another. There was a kind of 'yes' feeling and a strong team spirit.

7

The new customer engagement model: positive temptation towards mutual profit zone

After an extensive online dating process, the customer will want to meet their trusted adviser in person. They will want to confirm that their choice will bear fruit and

7

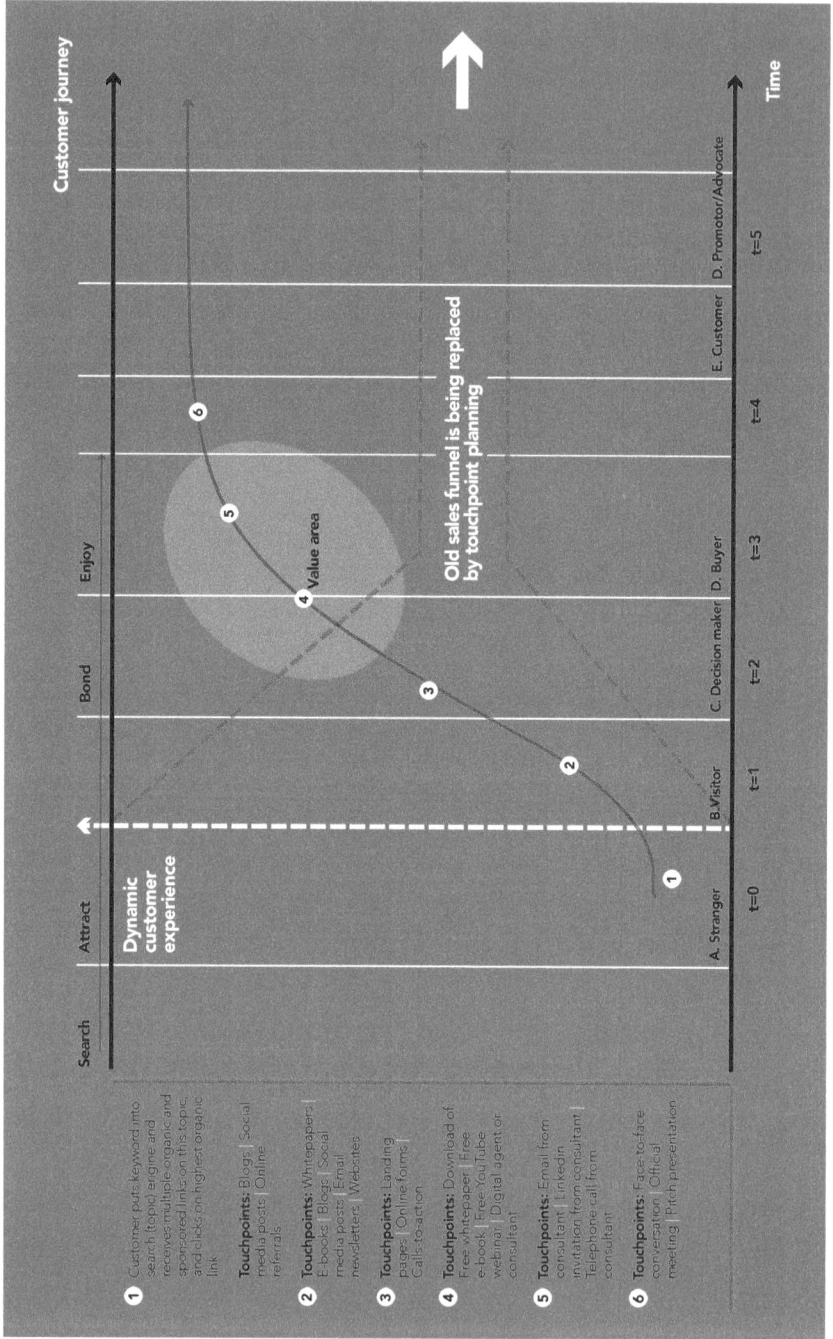

Figure 6 The new B2B customer engagement model

lead to success in the future. Figure 6 shows the role the consultative engagement approach plays in decision making in more depth:

- The Y-axis represents the customer experience;
- The X-axis shows 4 phases of the customer journey over time and 6 different roles a buyer can play.

Note: these phases may sometimes only take 1 or 2 touchpoints or the entire process could cover a period of one year and multiple touchpoints. It is important to go through each of these phases with the customer via retargeting. It should also be noted that there is no selling involved at all at in this process.

The goal is to eventually maximise the customer's interest or benefits (the curved line) - within the so-called value area - by saying or doing the right things in each phase. It is often the case that the result of a first discussion is a quotation. The question is whether the customer actually wanted one, or if they were just interested in getting an indication of prices. Experience has taught that it is often the latter and that sales teams spend hours producing unnecessary documents. This is a waste of time, as the chances of this document resulting in an actual sale are relatively low. A simple email is enough. Only 2–5% of all customer contacts result in a deal being signed. This means that the number of leads needs to be substantial in order to generate sufficient future sales. After all, in life it can also take several relationships before you find your *true love*.

Conclusion

The elite position of the traditional sales representative as the only person able to sell is long gone. (If this is not the case in your organisation, then perhaps you should read this chapter again!). Organisations now have an opportunity to deploy all of their personnel resources to create a new journey with prospective clients, where trust and authority (in terms of expertise) are playing an increasingly important role. The days of the hard sell are over. So, as in a personal relationship, first invest in building up engagement, trust and then follow careful steps towards the *commercial altar*: the sale, followed by a long and happy marriage.

7

CHAPTER 8

Strategic marketing planning

An agile strategy roadmap

The key to successful B2B marketing appears to lie in getting a highly motivated team on board to realise your strategic goals. In this chapter, I recall my early days as a young and enthusiastic marketing and sales manager at Vodafone. I will also explain the role the roadmap can play in internal communications and how it enabled my bosses to bring about a revolution in the Dutch mobile phone market. The roadmap template included at the end of this chapter (and available online) will help you clarify your direction, and ensure that your whole team understands where you're heading and equally importantly why. Ultimately this will enable you to be as successful as Vodafone in beating the competition.

It is no mean feat when a complete newcomer tries to enter a market that has been dominated by a monopolist for decades. Yet Libertel (now Vodafone) managed to rattle the cage of monopolist PTT Telecom (now KPN) considerably at the end of the last century, taking a 30% share of the market. And they didn't care how this was done. As employee number 134 and somewhat the *new kid on the block*, I witnessed the early days of the telecom pioneer first hand.

David slaying Goliath

From his perspective of self-management, wholeness and evolutionary purpose, international organisation and strategy consultant Frederic Laloux would these days call this *employee power*. I recall that this sense of evolutionary purpose, in particular, was felt strongly by me and my colleagues. It was a feeling that, as *team David*, we were actually slaying *Goliath*. We fought for lower telephone charges, so that mobile phones could be available for everyone. We fought for better provision of telecom services for all consumers and companies across the Netherlands. In those days, it was normal for PTT customers to wait a week for a new connection and that an employee at the call-centre could say "no" if you asked to be disconnected. Fortunately, that kind of customer experience is very much in the past.

8

After a couple of years, we discovered that not all our ambitions could be achieved with evolutionary purpose and entrepreneurialism alone. Moreover our new shareholder Vodafone was following our actions closely. We desperately needed a strategy roadmap.

Make your strategy a treasure map for all to see

The question that Libertel general management faced during this chaotic start-up was: how can I get all my employees to follow the same route on our company's roadmap in order to realise our goals? The solution for Libertel lay in the early 1990s invention by Robert Kaplan and David Norton: the balanced scorecard. The card hung as a poster at Libertel, in the corridor, near the management offices. Looking at it close-up, it looks like a fishbone (figure 7).

The main bone describes the customer journey and divides the marketing and sales process into smaller sub-steps or touchpoints (grey areas A through H). in the form of specific instructions.

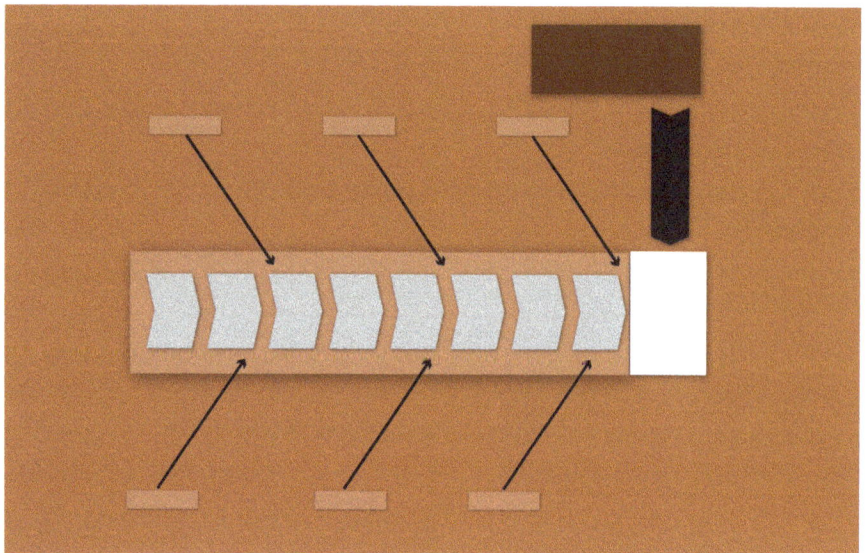

Figure 7 The Libertel scorecard as I remember it

These could be, for example:

A. sales assistant: phone potential customers;

B. corporate account manager: make appointment with client;

C. CRM employee: enter in customer details in the CRM system;

D. sales team: send quotation…

through to;

H. service team: send customers proposal for renewing their contract.

This might seem logical at first glance, but it is handy to have these instructions written out as imperatives. It creates calm by providing an overview. It also gives anyone using it a roadmap against which to check the direction they are going. At Libertel, it was a reassuring guide that enabled us to plan – and control - our customer's journey with us. It gave us a sense of control over the customer as we journeyed towards the head of the fish on which our company goals and targets were written for all to see. It was our *treasure map*.

Our fish

I clearly recall the six large side bones (perspectives) slanting towards the main bone. They contained management terms along the lines of lead generation, employees' personal development and finance. There were various smaller side bones alongside with specific actions such as: Organise a 12-week training programme for our managers together with HR. The legend alongside the card stated that these smaller side bones were the necessary actions to make the strategy work. These were known as the critical success factors (CSF). Hence, as employees, we saw targets, processes and strategy translated into concrete steps. It was basically all about putting strategy into action. The final part of the image I recall was a kind of spreadsheet containing a critical performance indicator (KPI) per CSF. For example, the CSF for training included a success rate test.

The very top of the poster showed a box with the company's vision and mission (the dark brown box in the image). This is the *'Why'* behind the company. I remember how excited I was about our aim to provide everyone with a mobile phone at an affordable price and with excellent customer service. As a young manager I was totally on board and put my heart and soul into helping realise this noble aim.

8

Employee involvement in an agile roadmap

You may think that the notion of a corporate scorecard, on display for all to see, marks the end of individual employee power. Yet, at Libertel, this was far from the case. As middle managers, we were also given the freedom to adapt the scorecard to our own situation. This agile philosophy (agility means adaptability) meant I was able to go off and find a template for the poster that I could use for my own team strategy. I filled in how I saw things and then discussed the results with my team. Once we had fine-tuned it together, we turned the final result into a placemat for everyone to put on their desk. In less than a year, we were at the head of all the sales lists and were nominated for the best sales team at Libertel. We had succeeded in making our strategy tangible. Not only in the form of a simple placemat, but with soaring sales. Within 5 years, Libertel had exceeded all expectations and took almost a 30% market share from PTT Telecom. This provided an excellent foundation for the company's stock market launch in 1999.

What if you don't like fish?

For those of you who don't like my fish, you'll be pleased to know that the format of the roadmap is flexible. At Sabel Communicatie (a Dutch medium-sized PR agency) I remember we initially used the agile strategy roadmap mentioned above. And 10 years later, when managers wanted to reassess the company's raison d'être with the team, we took the Golden Circle format by Sinek as our guide.

"If you hire people just because they can do a job they'll work for money. But if you hire people who believe what you believe they work for you with blood and sweat and tears."

Simon Sinek, management guru and author

8

A dynamic process

Although the scorecards are given a prominent place in the organisation, they are not written in stone. Over time, each of the critical success factors (the small side fish bones) in the marketing strategy are reviewed and where necessary adapted. Colleagues should be encouraged to play an active part in this process by suggesting changes. The manager is merely the owner of the document; the person responsible for updating it and for implementing the changes. Monthly team meetings are the platform for team members to voice any objections to the proposed changes and only those changes that have been agreed make it onto the map. As part of the dynamic process, a copy of the new version of the placemat is given to each member of the team as an aide memoire of the common marketing strategy.

*"Ever since my early success with a roadmap,
I've been making colourful placemats at the start
of every business innovation project I manage."*

Bringing calm and direction

Ever since my early success with a roadmap, I've been making colourful placemats at the start of every business innovation project I manage. I've used this approach not only at Dutch road and water authority Rijkswaterstaat (RWS), but also at waste management and recycling provider Van Gansewinkel, Software Company Exact, various non-profit organisations, professional associations and when coaching numerous start-ups. RWS now uses this format for internal communications on its in-house *ideas management* programme and when starting up a new internal organisational structure. Before the era of the roadmap RWS had little sense of common direction. According to the internal RWS consultant responsible for rolling out the ideas management programme, the roadmap has brought calm and direction. The roadmap has turned the umpteenth management toy into an effective means of communication between the various lines and levels in the organisation. Employees not only use the map, they also add to it. And, as a result, are successfully implementing the clearly defined and highly visible strategy.

8

A simple 4-step approach

1 - Brainstorm
Consider why and how and what

2 - Structure
- Define mission, vision, purpose and SMART goals and objectives
- Categorise actions into 6 perspectives based on goals and objectives: process, customer, growth, financial and perspective of choice
- Formulate critical success factors as imperatives

3 - Visualise
Draw the customer journey in a clear and concise deliverable.

4 - Update and consult
your employees on a regular basis.

Mission, vision, purpose of the organisation, identity

Goals

SMART objectives
- 5 Max.

Customer journey touchpoints

Critical Succes Factor written as an imperative

Perspective 1

Perspective 2

Perspective 3

Perspective 4

Perspective 5

Perspective 6

Critical succes factor written as an imperative

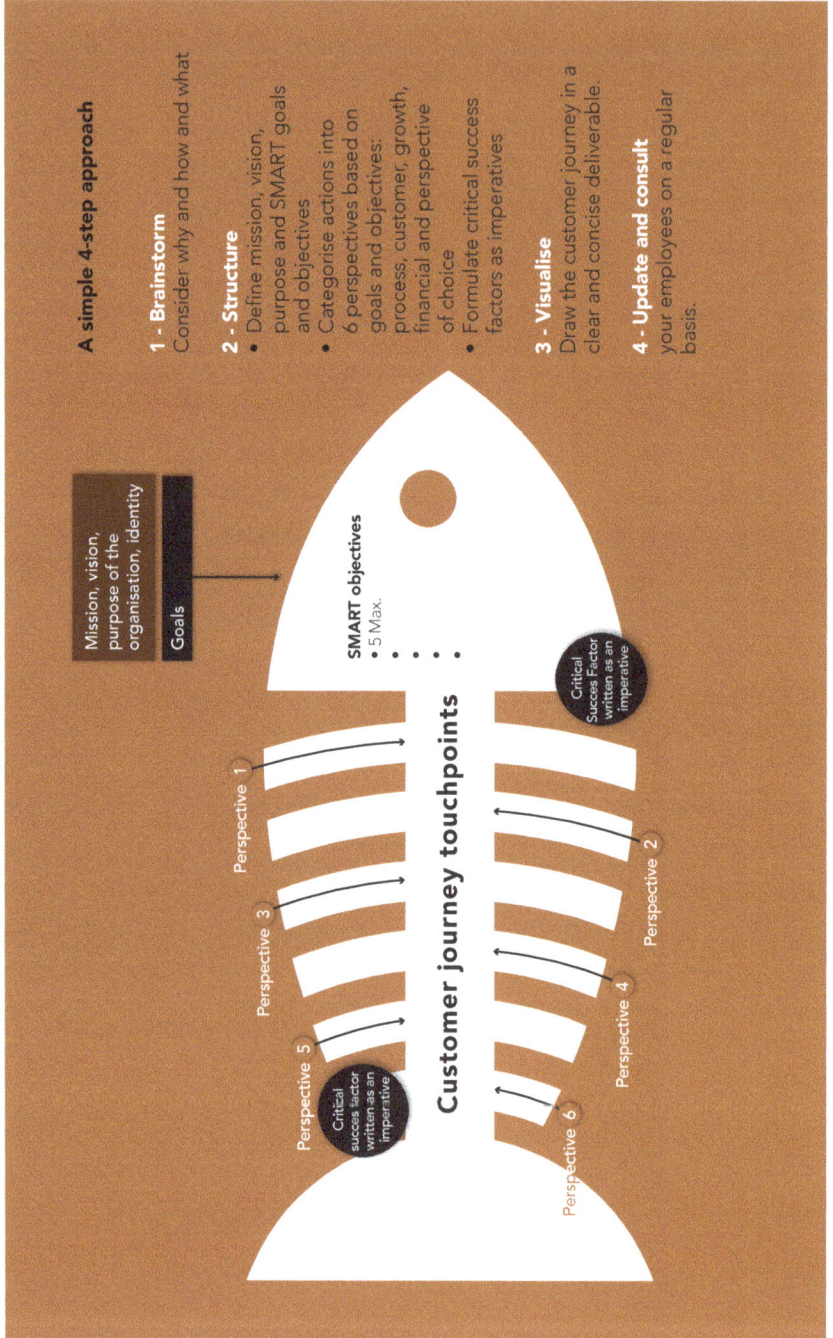

Figure 8 The agile marketing strategy roadmap

8

How to create your own agile marketing strategy roadmap

Step 1: Brainstorm about critical success factors

Organise a couple of informal and open brainstorm sessions with your team, customers and possible partners about the evolutionary purpose of the organisation (see Osterwalder or Sinek for ideas e.g. elaborate on the Why? How? and What?). At Sabel Communicatie I used flip-over sheets spread across six tables. The team would sit back with their feet up and share amusing anecdotes, stories, experiences and insights from the past year. Write everything down thoroughly, as these insights will become critical success factors for your business in the future.

Those who prefer gamification could opt for a core value game. For example, divide the group into two. One group starts with a set of cards with the current core values and the other with a set of completely new core values. It is important to ask a relevant question per table beforehand. For example: how does the company position itself in the market, what is its reputation and image, what are the core values, why are we involved in this together? One person per table should take notes and present the results at the end of the session. These critical success factor outputs could, for example, be presented on sticky-notes posted onto the wall.

Another method is the *IST to SOLL* method (German for the current situation 'Ist' and the future desired situation 'Soll'). Here, participants are interviewed individually in-depth about how they view the organisation now and what they expect from the organisation in the future. The chair classifies all the answers on the basis of a maximum of six perspectives (for example: financial, process, customer, innovation, human resource management, and marketing and communication, but others are also possible). The same chairperson then links the critical success factors given by the interviewee to these different perspectives.

Step 2: Introduce structure and create the roadmap

A. Write up the mission, vision, purpose, goals and objectives in the template
First, before you start creating your new concept roadmap, you should use the input from Step 1 to formulate (or update) your mission and vision statements. In other

8

97

words the purpose of your endeavours. If you are happy with your existing statements, enter these.

Secondly, enter your goals and objectives into the roadmap (see top right figure 8). Goals can be long term and less SMART than specific short-term objectives, which need to be as clear and detailed as possible. People always ask me how many goals or objectives they should come up with. Of course, this depends on the complexity of the business but you should have at least three or four of each.

B. The categories: structure marketing information into six perspectives

You now need to categorise and structure the input you have acquired into six perspectives. While this is something I love doing, I know that it's not everyone's cup of tea. But it is important to get this right, because otherwise you will not be able to focus your strategy and you will end up running in circles without achieving your goals.

First, categorise all of the information you gathered during Step 1 using keywords and organise these according to the six perspectives you came up with earlier. Which notes belong together? Which mean the same thing? Can you group the words in terms of common marketing denominators? For example:

- customer experience;
- customer satisfaction;
- branding;
- customer retention;
- marketing innovation;
- co-creation;
- market research;
- marketing communication
- positioning;
- targeting.

8

Secondly, start making choices by identifying which category is important and which is not, as well as which information is not yet a priority. Whenever I do this, it always reminds me of a game of *memory* with my youngest son. After a while, I really enjoy seeing the first contours appearing in the roadmap. This exercise is about finding focus and structure in your thinking, rather than being complete. Don't worry about leaving content out at this stage. You can save everything on your computer and access it later if you need to.

Thirdly, organise financial or budget information under one perspective. The same applies to everything related to HR. Map these onto the far-left of your roadmap. Be sure not to forget these items as every organisation needs budget and staffing!

C. Make imperatives of the critical success factors for each of the six perspectives

The next step is to add the critical success factors you collected during Step 1 as imperatives. You may wonder why you need an imperative here. The explanation that I was once given by former Vodafone's managing director, Hans van Veen, is simple: people who work for you like to have clear guidelines and instructions on what you expect from them, rather than vague *Shall we…?* questions. In contrast, I notice that a lot of managers are actually afraid of giving clear instructions in an imperative style because they fear they will be disliked by their staff. However, management and staff do not have to be to be *best friends.* Instead, management has the task of communicating as clearly as possible. This roadmap is a perfect means for you to convey your strategy and its implications to your employees.

Having identified the critical success factors, first rewrite each one as a specific instruction. For example, the interviewee tells you that in the category customer satisfaction, it is critical to reward loyal customers with a VIP invitation to an annual event. On your roadmap, this becomes the imperative: *Invite loyal customers to VIP event every year.*

Secondly, you need to group these instructions under the six larger side bones you defined earlier. That is, add them to your roadmap on one of the six perspectives. Here too, the plotting is based on logic, your own judgement and creativity. Once again don't worry about getting it perfect. You can always re-arrange the items later, if necessary.

8

Step 3: Define the customer journey and touchpoint planning

As an attentive reader, you have probably realised that there is still a large empty area in the middle of the template. I have saved this perspective till last because it creates space for the different steps on the customer journey, that is, the different *touchpoints* with the customer. Every perspective and critical success factor on the roadmap needs to contribute to the customer journey and to optimising the touchpoints. If this is not the case with a specific item, then remove it immediately because otherwise it will distract you from reaching your marketing goals.

Finally, take a look at your roadmap. Check again that every tag, item, and perspective will help you realise an optimal customer journey. Now ask yourself: Does the customer journey you have specified, lead you towards achieving your marketing goals and objectives? And is everything aligned with the purpose of your business? If the answer to all of these points is yes, then congratulations! You have created your first agile marketing strategy roadmap.

Step 4: Hang up your roadmap and re-evaluate it regularly

Strategy is a crucial element in business practice and needs to be alive in your daily operations. So, the final phase is to use the roadmap as a visual communication tool for your employees. I suggest you hang it up on your office wall, for example. Or use it as a recurring internal social media or intranet item. You also need to re-evaluate your roadmap regularly so that it maintains it's relevance and continues to play it's fundamental, dynamic role in your organisation. Talk about it in your weekly meetings. But, above all, don't make the fatal mistake of leaving it in your desk drawer! Why not make it into a placemat, for example, instead?

8

Conclusion

Agile marketing strategy mapping, including touchpoint planning, is the cornerstone of managing the customer journey. It will help marketers to align marketing strategy to an optimal customer experience based on the overall corporate strategy and corporate goals. It will also help marketing managers justify their efforts to management. The template I have shown you is an example of a format that has worked very well for me on numerous occasions. There are other tools and approaches available. But their aims are the same: clear communication as to where you're heading and why. If you can show the way, your team will join you on creating a great customer journey along the right road.

8

CONCLUSION

Moving on

To responsible influencing using customer centred signalling

The journey I have described in this book started in Australia twenty years ago. It brought us to many different B2B market-places all over the world. Now as our journey is coming to an end it is clear that the B2B marketing and sales profession is struggling to stay relevant. There are four reasons for this.

Firstly, the new decision making unit is the internet. Therefore, new internet-based technologies have shifted the balance of power away from the marketer and sales-man towards the buyer.

Secondly, today's management and organisational consultants claim that the future of B2B marketing boils down to simply doing what feels good and offering products that make employees proud of themselves. This general lack of insight into the need for a more scientific approach of marketing is not being addressed and countered enough in business schools. Take Frederic Laloux' management book Reinventing Organisations for example. An influential management book that is used to teach new generations. Only three paragraphs are dedicated to marketing, reducing B2B marketing almost to non-existent proportions. In fact Laloux questions the future role of marketing altogether. Maybe that is not so strange, if you picture my ball pit once again. It seems that not only marketers but also scientists are experiencing social and online media (the new DMU) to be a bit chaotic. The balls seem to be constantly flying around the room and never landing in the pit at all. But that is not the case: people still end up buying things and going through a decision making process. It is up to researchers and marketing as a science to keep up with these developments.

Thirdly, it is not surprising that marketers are experiencing more and more difficul-ties in meeting management needs, because they are not being provided with new theories, models and insights into the changing seller-buyer relationship. Neither are they equipped to show which strategic marketing plans have an effect on B2B buying and bring results. It has become impossible to show direct links between their mar-keting strategy efforts and sales.

C

Finally, increased internet and social media usage in B2B have decreased information asymmetries between buyer and seller, and buyers experiencing more freedom in their customer journey because of it.

The changing landscape, and how to stay relevant as a profession

The changing landscape of B2B buying is the policy aspect that concerns managers most. As a result, understanding B2B buying behaviour is a top priority topic for advancing B2B marketing and keeping your business in a profitable market position. B2B marketing must look for ways in which you can build brand confidence on social media. Using social media influencers that are more authentic and that appeal to the new generation B2B buyers. In other words it is key for B2B marketers to use responsible influencing that is based on customer centred signalling.

In order to be able to that, you must measure the DCE (dynamic customer experience) constantly via marketing research. As well as invest in thorough touchpoint planning, stakeholder management and reputational tracking. Marketeers must map the customer journey with the new customer engagement model that has been introduced in this book and periodically update their agile strategy roadmap.

Sales and marketing professionals beware!

If you are a sales and marketing professional, you will have noticed that someone has moved the goalposts. Whether it's a colleague who posted a blog without checking with you first, or a satisfied customer singing the praises of your product in a LinkedIn group. You no longer control what is said about your brand and by whom. Fancy brand messages and style guides, designed to ensure the entire organisation is singing from the same hymn sheet when it comes to features, benefits, core values etc. are all becoming less relevant. As are those individuals who set them in stone and guard them behind lock and key. The interaction process with the customer is no longer solely your domain but takes place on multiple touchpoints. Your customer is screening every one of your signals with scepticism and transforming them into a dynamic customer experience (DCE). Thus, to be able to follow your customer on their journey you will need to remember the following points (and don't worry I'll help you).

C

- To start working on your touchpoint planning and multiply them.
- To design a new algorithm to be able to calculate real-time DCE.
- To transform your online marketing strategy from content selling, inbound marketing and marketing automation to responsible influencing based on customer centred signalling strategy.
- To install real-time reputation management.
- To empower your employees to becoming social influencers.
- To work with an agile marketing roadmap that helps you stay on track.

In fact, if you fail to respond to these changes, you may find yourself unable to bridge the buyer-seller gap all together. Your customers are on a journey. En route they call in at lots of ports, places and river crossings. These touchpoints are many and varied. You need to identify them and use them wisely – either yourself as booster or champion, or via third party social influencers - and help your customers to make their way across the bridge over the buyer-seller gap.

As mentioned before I have no commercial interest in selling you this book, but am happy to take any donation in exchange for a copy of this book to be able to continue this independent research in the coming three years. My ultimate goal is to gain a PhD degree in this field. I will use this newly acquired knowledge to share it freely with you and in my classrooms.

Please visit signallingthebook.com for further information on how to donate.

Bibliography

Abidin, C. (2015). Micro-microcelebrity: Branding babies on the Internet. (M. Journal, Producer) From http://journal.media culture.org.au/index.php/mcjournal/article/view/1022

Arndt, J. (1967). Role of product-related conversations in the diffusion of a new product. *Journal of marketing Research*, 291-295.

Arthurs, J. D., Busenitz, L. W., Hoskisson, R. E., & Johnson, R. A. (2009). Signaling and initial public offerings: The use and impact of the lockup period. Journal of Business Venturing, 24(4), 360-372.

Bandura, A. (2012). Semiotics. In E. Griffin, A first look at communication theory (Vol. 8, p. 356). New York: MGraw Hill Companies, Inc.

Bhargava, H. K., & Choudhary, V. (2001). Information goods and vertical differentiation. Journal of Management Information Systems, 18(2), 89-106.

Binkley M., Stand Out: How to Quit Cold Calling and Use Social Media For B2B Sales. http://sleepingbarber.com/wp-content/uploads/2012/11/STAND-OUT.pdf (2012)

Birkigt, K., Stadler, M. M., & Funck, H. J. (1998). Corporate identity: grundlagen, funktionen, fallbeispiele. MI Wirtschaftsbuch.

Booth, N., & Matic, J. A. (2011). Mapping and leveraging influencers in social media to shape corporate brand perceptions. *Corporate Communications: An International Journal*, 16(3), 184-191.

Busenitz, L. W., Fiet, J. O., & Moesel, D. D. (2005). Signaling in Venture Capitalist—New Venture Team Funding Decisions: Does It Indicate Long-Term Venture Outcomes? Entrepreneurship Theory and Practice, 29(1), 1-12.

Chandran, S., & Morwitz, V. G. (2006). The price of "free"-dom: Consumer sensitivity to promotions with negative contextual influences. Journal of consumer research, 33(3), 384-392.

Chung, W., & Kalnins, A. (2001). Agglomeration effects and performance: A test of the Texas lodging industry. Strategic Management Journal, 22(10), 969-988.

Cialdini, R. B., & Rhoads, K. V. (2001). Human behavior and the marketplace. Marketing Research, 13(3), 8.

Connelly, B. L., Certo, S. T., Ireland, R. D., & Reutzel, C. R. (2011). Signaling theory: A review and assessment. Journal of Management, 37(1), 39-67.

Council, M. L. (2012). The digital evolution in B2B marketing. The Corporate Executive Board Company www. mlc. executive board. com (assessed November 2014).

Davenport, T. H., Leibold, M., & Voelpel, S. C. (2007). Strategic management in the innovation economy: Strategic approaches and tools for dynamic innovation capabilities. John Wiley & Sons.

Durcikova, A., & Gray, P. (2009). How Knowledge Validation Processes Affect Knowledge Contribution. Journal of Management Information Systems, 25(4), 81-108.

Dwyer, F. R., & Walker Jr, O. C. (1981). Bargaining in an asymmetrical power structure. The Journal of Marketing, 104-115.

Fombrun, C. J., & Van Riel, C. B. M. (2003). Fame & fortune: How the world's top companies develop winning reputations. Pearson Education.

Freberg, K., Graham, K., McGaugey, K., & Freberg, L. A. (2010). Who are the social media influencers? A study of public perceptions of personality. Elsevier Inc.

Friestad, M., & Wright, P. (1994). The persuasion knowledge model: How people cope with persuasion attempts. Journal of consumer research, 21(1), 1-31.

Gomulya, D., & Mishina, Y. (2016). Signaler credibility, signal susceptibility, and relative reliance on signals: How stakeholders change their evaluative processes after violation of expectations and rehabilitative efforts. Academy of Management Journal, amj. 2014.1041.

Grazer, B., Howard, R., Goldsman, A., Crowe, R., Harris, E., Connelly, J., Bettany, P., ... Imagine Entertainment (Firm). (2002). A beautiful mind. Willowdale, Ont: Distributed by Universal Studios Canada.

Grewal, R., Lilien, G. L., Bharadwaj, S., Jindal, P., Kayande, U., Lusch, R. F., . . . Scheer, L. K. (2015). Business-to-business buying: challenges and opportunities. Customer needs and Solutions, 2(3), 193-208.

Ippolito, P. M. (1990). Bonding and nonbonding signals of product quality. Journal of Business, 41-60.

Kaplan, Robert S., & David P. Norton. (1996).

Kaplan, R. S., & Norton, D. P. (1996). The balanced scorecard: translating strategy into action. Harvard Business Press.

Karpoff, J. M., Lee, D. S., & Martin, G. S. (2008). The cost to firms of cooking the books. Journal of Financial and Quantitative Analysis, 43(03), 581-611.

Kirmani, A., & Rao, A. R. (2000). No pain, no gain: A critical review of the literature on signaling unobservable product quality. Journal of Marketing, 64(2), 66-79.

Kranzbühler, A. M., Kleijnen, M. H., Morgan, R. E., & Teerling, M. (2017). The Multilevel Nature of Customer Experience Research: An Integrative Review and Research Agenda. International Journal of Management Reviews.

Kurtz, G., Brackett, L., Kasdan, L., Kershner, I., Lucas, G., Hamill, M., Ford, H., ... Twentieth Century Fox Home Entertainment, Inc. (2004). Star Wars: Episode V. United States: 20th Century Fox.

Lacka, E., & Chong, A. (2016). Usability perspective on social media sites' adoption in the B2B context. Industrial Marketing Management, 54, 80-91.

Laloux, F. (2014). Reinventing organizations: A guide to creating organizations inspired by the next stage in human consciousness. Nelson Parker.

Lambrecht, A., & Misra, K. (2016). Fee or Free: When Should Firms Charge for Online Content? Management Science, 63(4), 1150-1165.

Lambrecht, A., & Tucker, C. (2013). When does retargeting work? Information specificity in online advertising. Journal of Marketing Research, 50(5), 561-576.

Lanzolla, G., & Frankort, H. T. (2016). The Online Shadow of Offline Signals: Which Sellers Get Contacted in Online B2B Marketplaces? Academy of Management Journal, 59(1), 207-231.

Lee, M., & Yuon, S. (2009). Electronic Word of Mouth (eWoM). In International Journal of Advertising (pp. 473-499).

Lilien, G. L. (2016). The B2B knowledge gap. International Journal of Research in Marketing, 33(3), 543-556.

Lilien, G. L., & Grewal, R. (Eds.). (2012). Handbook on business to business marketing. Edward Elgar Publishing.

Litvin, S., Goldsmith, R., & Pan, B. (2008). Electronic word of mouth in hospitality and tourism management. In Tourism Management (Vol. 3, pp. 458-468).

McGovern, G. (2016). NEW THINKING: The organization of the customer. E-mail Newsletter. 27th of March.

Miller, Arthur, 1915-2005. (1996). Death of a salesman. New York :Penguin Books,. Chicago. Miller, Arthur, 1915-2005.

Scott, D. M. (2015). The new rules of marketing and PR: How to use social media, online video, mobile applications, blogs, news releases, and viral marketing to reach buyers directly. John Wiley & Sons.

Simpson, D., Bruckheimer, J., Scott, T., Cash, J., Epps, J., Cruise, T., McGillis, K., ... Paramount Pictures Corporation. (2004). Top gun. Hollywood, Calif: Paramount Home Entertainment.

Milgram Experiment - Big History NL, threshold 6 (www.youtube.com/watch?v=xOYLCy5PVgM)

Milgram, S. (1963). Behavioral study of obedience. Journal of Abnormal and Social Psychology, 67, 371-378.

Narayandas, D. (2005). Building loyalty in business markets. Harvard Business Review, 83(9), 131-139.

Narayandas, D., & Rangan, V. K. (2004). Building and sustaining buyer–seller relationships in mature industrial markets. Journal of Marketing, 68(3), 63-77.

Nielsen's Global Trust in Advertising Survey (2012) http://www.nielsen.com/us/en/insights/reports/2012/global-trust-in-advertising-and-brand-messages.html

Osterwalder, A., & Pigneur, Y. (2010). Business model generation: a handbook for visionaries, game changers, and challengers. John Wiley & Sons.

Pulizzi, J. (2016). 2016_B2B_Content Marketing Final. Content Marketing Institute. http://contentmarketinginstitute.com/wp-content/uploads/2016/09/2017_B2B_Research_FINAL.pdf

Rhee, M., & Haunschild, P. R. (2006). The liability of good reputation: A study of product recalls in the US automobile industry. Organization Science, 17(1), 101-117.

Sanders, W., & Boivie, S. (2004). Sorting things out: Valuation of new firms in uncertain markets. Strategic Management Journal, 25(2), 167-186.

Scorsese, M., Winter, T., DiCaprio, L., Aziz, R., McFarland, J., Koskoff, E. T., Kacandes, G., ... EMJAG Productions. (2014). The Wolf of Wall Street.

Sethuraman R., Tellis G.J., & Briesch R.A. (2011). How well does advertising work? Generalizations from meta-analysis of brand advertising elasticities. Journal Of Marketing Research, 48(3), 457-471.

Shampanier, K., Mazar, N., & Ariely, D. (2007). Zero as a special price: The true value of free products. Marketing science, 26(6), 742-757.

Shapiro, C., & Varian, H. R. (1998). Versioning: the smart way to. Harvard Business Review, 107(6), 107.

Sinek, S., (2009), Start with Why: How Great Leaders Inspire Everyone to Take Action

Spence, A. M. (1974). Market signaling: Informational transfer in hiring and related screening processes (Vol. 143): Harvard University Press.

Spence, M. (1973). Job market signaling. The quarterly journal of Economics, 87(3), 355-374.

Spence, M. (2002). Signaling in retrospect and the informational structure of markets. The American Economic Review, 92(3), 434-459.

Srivastava, J. (2001). The role of inferences in sequential bargaining with one-sided incomplete information: Some experimental evidence. Organizational behavior and human decision processes, 85(1), 166-187.

Steenburgh, T. J., Avery, J., Dahod, N., & Harvard Business School. (2011). HubSpot: Inbound marketing and Web 2.0 (Rev: January 24, 2011.). ([HBS case collection]). Boston, MA: Harvard Business School Publishing.

Stiglitz, J. E. (2000). The contributions of the economics of information to twentieth century economics. Quarterly Journal of economics, 1441-1478.

Strong Jr, E. K. (1925). Theories of selling. Journal of applied psychology, 9(1), 75.

Swani, K., Brown, B. P., & Milne, G. R. (2014). Should tweets differ for B2B and B2C? An analysis of Fortune 500 companies' Twitter communications. Industrial Marketing Management, 43(5), 873-881.

Vargo, S. L., & Lusch, R. F. (2004). Evolving to a New Dominant Logic for Marketing. Journal Of Marketing, 68(1), 1-17.

Verlegh, P.W.J., (2015). Marketeers en consumenten: Samen spelen, samen delen. Vrije Universiteit Amsterdam. Inaugural speech upon accepting the position of Professor of Marketing at the Faculty of Economics and Business Administration.

Wiersema, F. (2013). The B2B agenda: The current state of B2B marketing and a look ahead.

Zavyalova, A., Pfarrer, M. D., Reger, R. K., & Shapiro, D. L. (2012). Managing the message: The effects of firm actions and industry spillovers on media coverage following wrongdoing. Academy of Management Journal, 55(5), 1079-1101.

Zeithaml, V. A. (1988). Consumer perceptions of price, quality, and value: a means-end model and synthesis of evidence. The Journal of Marketing, 2-22.

Omissions

Every effort has been taken by the author to identify all sources used in this book. If you believe an omission has been made, please inform the publisher immediately.

About the author

Klaas Fleischmann MSc (1971) holds a first-class degree in Economics, Business Administration & Marketing from Maastricht University as well as a post-graduate diploma
in Journalism from the Erasmus University Rotterdam. He is currently a PhD candidate
at the School of Business and Economics of the VU Amsterdam, where he is carrying
out research into the digitalisation of the B2B customer decision journey. He is also a
lecturer in marketing at the HU University of Applied Sciences Utrecht. He lives with his
wife and their 3 sons in Utrecht in the Netherlands.

Recommendations

"Whether he's trying to develop a customer relationship or solve a communications
challenge, Fleischmann is both methodical and tenacious".
Christiaan Lustig, Lead consultant and managing partner, Brayton House

"Thank you for introducing me to the 'signalling theory' in marketing! I'm inspired by
Klaas' contribution and his extensive expertise and skills in corporate communication,
marketing and journalism." This book is just one example of him sharing his knowledge
and insight. Enjoy!"
*Ari Purnama, Researcher and Lecturer in Communication & Media, University of
Groningen*

"Klaas Fleischmann's writing is one with an unflappable, positive attitude. He is full of
drive and energy, and never gives up. Over the years I have seen his entrepreneurial
skills unfold and develop, making him highly successful in his chosen field of work".
Peter Søndergaard Sørensen, Sales Consultant

www.ingramcontent.com/pod-product-compliance
Lightning Source LLC
Chambersburg PA
CBHW080133240326
41458CB00128B/6355